DELICIOUS
DESSERTS

DELICIOUS
DESSERTS

Jane Suthering

CONTENTS

INTRODUCTION
PAGE 6

QUICK AND EASY
PAGE 12

COLD DESSERTS
PAGE 22

SPECIAL OCCASIONS
PAGE 40

HOT PUDDINGS
PAGE 56

FROZEN DESSERTS
PAGE 70

INDEX
PAGE 80

Published exclusively for Marks and Spencer plc
in 1983 by Octopus Books Limited
59 Grosvenor Street, London W1

© 1983 Hennerwood Publications Limited

ISBN 0 86273 066 X

Produced by Mandarin Publishers Ltd
22a Westlands Road
Quarry Bay
Hong Kong

Printed in Hong Kong

INTRODUCTION

This book is divided into five chapters, comprising a Quick and Easy section; Cold Desserts; Special Occasion Desserts; Hot Puddings and Frozen Desserts. Although there is a theme to each chapter, many basic mixtures, including pastry, meringue, egg custards and creamed or whisked sponges may be found in more than one section.

Quick and Easy

As the name implies, this section includes desserts which can be put together simply and easily. Some may be almost 'instant'; many are based on fresh whipped cream with added flavourings, such as Strawberry and Cointreau Crush, Scottish Honey Possett and Honeycomb Fool. Fresh and canned fruits are very useful and can be served in a variety of ways, for example, to accompany sweetened fried bread for Apricot Toasts. Liqueurs and wine marry very successfully with fruits to give delicious results, as in Banana Flambé and Cherries in Red Wine. Jelly-based desserts, whether using a jelly tablet or gelatine, are always quick and easy to make although time is required to set them. Melon combines well with a grapefruit jelly to give a refreshing dessert and Rhubarb Mallow makes good use of store cupboard ingredients to make an interesting dessert for unexpected guests.

Cold Desserts

This chapter includes the preparation of egg custards, for which the basic ingredients are eggs and milk or cream. Crème Brûlée is a rich spoonable custard with a caramel crust whilst Crème Caramel is a firm custard which is baked and then unmoulded. Pouring custard is included in Floating Islands and a rich egg custard makes up the additional filling for French Apple Tart. Fresh fruit always makes a good dessert, especially if it is prepared with imagination. The Pineapple and Kirsch Roll, for example, makes a spectacular use of a fresh pineapple.

Canned or frozen fruits are always useful to make mousses and other foam puddings, for example, Gooseberry Fool and Blackcurrant Whip. Soft cheeses, such as cream, curd or cottage cheese are good standbys for making cheesecakes, but try Paskha or Fromage à la Crème for an unusual variation. This section also uses a variety of pastries, from shortcrust and frozen puff pastry to rich sweet pastries and strudel. Egg white is used in a variety of ways: to make meringues which can be baked or poached in milk for Floating Islands or simply beaten to add lightness to mousses and fools.

Special Occasion Desserts

This chapter includes desserts which may take some time to prepare, assemble and decorate, but it is well worth taking a little extra time to produce a spectacular result. Some are quite inexpensive, using basic ingredients with perhaps a special seasonal fruit, for example, the Nectarine Vacherin and Kiwi Fruit Pavlova, both variations of meringue decorated with whipped cream and exotic fruit. If the fruit suggested in the recipe is difficult to buy, experiment with other flavours. Most fresh fruit can be used, or use well-drained canned fruit. Liqueurs and spirits are used frequently in this chapter to enhance and complement the flavour of the desserts and to add a touch of sparkle.

Hot Puddings

To most people the thought of hot puddings usually conjures up steamed syrup pudding or jam roly-poly. This section does offer a few such traditional favourites, for example, Sussex Pond Pudding, a suet crust encasing a buttery lemon filling with a whole lemon in the centre, Plum Dumplings and various steamed sponge desserts. It also gives some new ideas for using basic ingredients. New York Noodle Pudding, for example, uses ribbon pasta in a rich egg custard as an alternative to rice. French Plum Pudding is made like an upside-down pudding and is turned out to show an attractive arrangement of fruit. For Surprise Lemon Pudding, the sponge mixture is cooked in such a way that it separates to give a golden sponge crust with a tangy lemon sauce beneath.

Frozen Desserts

Frozen desserts are always a bonus when you are faced with unexpected guests or if extra time is needed to prepare a main course. This section contains recipes which can be served straight from the freezer and those which need time to soften in the refrigerator before serving. All ice creams, water ices and sorbets will scoop better if allowed to soften slightly. The exact time will depend on the mixture, but it will probably be anything from 15 minutes to one hour. If the mixture is frozen in a shaped mould, for example, the Coffee and Hazelnut Ice Cream Cake or Biscuit Tortoni, the dessert can be unmoulded on to a serving plate and returned to the freezer to firm up before decorating. Iced Zabaglione, and Chocolate Rum Cake can all be served straight from the freezer, as the combination of ingredients stops the mixtures from freezing solid.

The recipes in this book cover a wide range of preparations; the list of hints below will help you to produce the best results.

Cream

Single cream will not whip but can be used as pouring cream to serve with desserts. Whipping cream or double cream have a much greater fat content and can therefore be beaten. Whipping cream will only give soft peaks and is useful for spooning on top of desserts or to sandwich layers together such as the meringue discs for the Nectarine Vacherin or the crisp biscuit layers for Cinnamon Galette. Double cream can be beaten until stiff enough for piping. Take care not to overwhip the cream which will give an unattractive granular consistency. Correctly whipped cream should have a smooth texture and stand in peaks when the whisk is lifted from the bowl.

Making Purées

The quickest and easiest way to purée fruit is to use a liquidizer and then to pass the purée through a sieve to remove seeds, pips, and stringy fibres. However, pushing the fruit through a sieve with the back of a wooden spoon or pestle is just as effective, only a little more time-consuming.

Preparing Nuts

The tough outer skin of nuts should always be removed before using them in desserts. Almonds and hazelnuts are often sold ready-skinned (blanched) but are very easy to prepare yourself. For almonds and walnuts, cover the nuts with cold water, and bring to the boil. Strain, plunge the nuts in cold water, then strain again and remove the skins. For hazelnuts, place the nuts under a preheated grill for about 5 minutes, turning occasionally. Allow to cool slightly, then place the nuts in a paper bag or in a tea towel and rub them together to remove the papery skin. To toast nuts, either place them under a preheated grill, turning frequently, or in a medium hot oven for about 10 minutes until golden brown.

Working with Pastry

Always handle pastry as little as possible. After rolling out and lining a flan tin, cover, wrap and chill the pastry case for at least 30 minutes or leave it in the freezer until firm. This relaxes the pastry and helps prevent toughening. This is also a good idea for shaped pastries, such as the Mincemeat and Apple Jalousie or Gâteau Pithiviers. Flan cases are often 'baked blind' or precooked which helps prevent the filling from making the pastry soggy. If the filling is to be cooked, cover the pastry case with a circle of greaseproof paper, at least 7.5 cm (3 inches) larger than the diameter of the flan. Fill the case with 'baking beans', either manufactured ones or ordinary dried pulses. Bake the flan in a hot oven until the pastry has set, then remove the beans and paper and continue baking for a few more minutes to allow the pastry base to dry out. Flan cases may be par-cooked or fully cooked in this way. If the pastry case is to contain a cold filling, simply prick the pastry well with a fork and bake until golden brown.

When a weight of pastry is given in a recipe this refers to the amount of flour used and not to the total weight of the prepared pastry.

Steamed Puddings

If you don't own a steamer, the best method is to use a large saucepan in which the pudding basin can sit comfortably allowing about 5 cm (2 inch) gap between the basin and sides of the pan. Fill the pan with hot water to come about three-quarters of the way up the basin. Cover and simmer (steam) gently for the required time ensuring that the water level is checked from time to time.

Using Gelatine

It is always a good idea to soak gelatine in the measured amount of liquid specified in the recipe before dissolving it. To dissolve the gelatine and remove its granular texture, place the 'sponged' liquid in a small basin in a saucepan of hot water, or place it directly in the pan over very gentle heat until the liquid is clear. Do not allow it to boil as this will make the gelatine go 'ropey'. Make sure the gelatine-based mixture is on the point of setting (the consistency of egg white) before folding in other ingredients, for example, whipped cream or beaten egg whites, or chopped fruit. Unless the mixture is cool enough, the ingredients will not combine well and in the case of heavier ingredients, may sink.

Unmoulding Jellies or Ice Creams

Either fill a bowl with boiling water and dip the mould very quickly into boiling water and then invert it on to a plate, or soak a tea towel in boiling water, press out any excess water and wrap around the inverted mould. Carefully lift off the mould and return the jelly (or ice cream) to the fridge (or freezer) to firm. The surface of the dessert may have melted slightly on unmoulding. However, once the dessert has been allowed to firm up, any liquid on the serving plate will have solidified and can be scraped off with a knife.

Equipment

A few of the recipes in this book require specialized equipment such as a bombe mould (Hazelnut and Coffee Ice Cream Cake). However, a pudding basin or a cake tin of a similar capacity can be used instead. If you haven't got an ice cream scoop or a melon baller for serving ice cream, use a spoon. Loose-bottomed cake tins will double up as flan tins.

Decorating Ideas

The presentation of any pudding or dessert is always very important and there are many different types of decoration to choose from.

Citrus Fruits

Twists: Cut a thin slice of lemon, lime or orange, remove any pips and make a cut from the centre to the outside edge. Twist the two cut edges in opposite directions.
Butterflies: Take half slices of fruit and cut them almost in two, separate the two halves to give a butterfly shape.
Spirals: Using a canelle knife, vegetable peeler or small sharp knife, cut long strips of rind from the fruit and twist them into spirals.
Julienne strips: Using a vegetable peeler, pare the rind from the fruit and cut it into very fine strips. If wished, cover the strips with boiling water and leave for 5 minutes to preserve their colour and freshness and remove excess bitterness. Drain and leave in cold water until required.
Baskets: Make baskets from whole fruit by cutting the fruit in half, making a straight cut or zig zag edge and removing the flesh, or make baskets with handles (page 70).
Use small sprigs of mint or strawberry leaves, crystallized fruits cut into decorative shapes, chocolate or sugar 'coffee beans' or crystallized rose and violet petals with angelica stems. Create a border of piped cream shells or rosettes or swirl whipped cream with a fork. Melt chocolate in a bowl set over a pan of hot water and cool slightly. Drizzle the chocolate over a dessert from a spoon or pipe fine lines from a greaseproof piping bag (page 46) with a small hole cut in the end. Use chocolate curls (page 16), whole, flaked or chopped toasted nuts, caramel chips or praline (page 72).

1. Soufflé dish   2. Spring form cake tin   3. French fluted flan tin
4. Porcelain flan dish   5. Ramekins   6. Bombe mould   7. Charlotte
mould   8. Nylon piping bag   9. Paper piping bag   10. Piping nozzles
11. Cherry stoner   12. Canelle knife   13. Melon baller   14. Small palette
knife   15. Coeur à la crème moulds   16. Copper moulds

QUICK AND EASY

STRAWBERRY AND COINTREAU CRUSH

Serves 4-6
225 g (8 oz) strawberries, washed
2 tablespoons caster sugar
1-2 tablespoons Cointreau
250 ml (8 fl oz) double or whipping cream

Preparation time: 10 minutes, plus chilling

1. Reserve 4-6 small strawberries for decoration. Hull and roughly crush the remainder with the sugar.
2. Place the Cointreau and cream in a bowl and whip until stiff. Fold the strawberry mixture into the cream.
3. Spoon into individual glass dishes and top with slices of strawberry. Chill until required.

BLACKCURRANT FLUFF

1 x 425 g (15 oz) can blackcurrants
grated rind and juice of 1 medium orange
15 g (½ oz) gelatine
2 egg whites
50 g (2 oz) caster sugar
whipped cream, to decorate (optional)

Preparation time: 15 minutes, plus chilling

1. Place the blackcurrants with their syrup and half the orange rind in a liquidizer goblet. Blend to a purée.
2. Dissolve the gelatine in the orange juice in a bowl set over hot water. Stir into the blackcurrant purée. Chill until on the point of setting.
3. Whisk the egg whites to soft peaks then whisk in the sugar a little at a time until thick and glossy. Fold into the blackcurrant mixture.
4. Spoon the mixture into 4 individual dishes and chill until required.
5. Decorate with whipped cream and/or the remaining orange rind.

Variation:
Use 1 x 425 g (15 oz) can pineapple rings in natural juice in place of blackcurrants. Proceed as above.

MELON AND GRAPEFRUIT JELLY

Serves 6
1½ tablespoons gelatine
600 ml (1 pint) unsweetened grapefruit juice
1 honeydew melon, 1.25 kg (2½-2¾ lb), skinned and seeded
To decorate:
whipped cream or plain unsweetened yogurt (optional)
stem ginger (optional)

Preparation time: 20 minutes, plus setting

Home made jellies are so good and are completely different in flavour to those made with a commercial jelly tablet.

This recipe is particularly easy as the base is unsweetened fruit juice – use any fruit juice such as orange, pineapple, apple or grape or combinations of these with fresh fruits added to complement the flavour of the jelly. Always allow the jelly to partially set before adding the fruit otherwise the fruit is likely to stick to the bottom of the mould. This would produce two separate layers and not an even distribution of jelly and fruit.

1. Dissolve the gelatine in 6 tablespoons of grapefruit juice over gentle heat. Stir in the remaining juice and chill until it is the consistency of egg white.
2. Roughly chop the melon flesh. Stir into the jelly.
3. Spoon the mixture into a 1.2 litre (2 pint) jelly mould. Chill until set.
4. Unmould and decorate with cream or yogurt and slices of stem ginger, (if using).

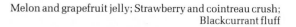

Melon and grapefruit jelly; Strawberry and cointreau crush; Blackcurrant fluff

PINEAPPLE AND KIRSCH ROLL

Serves 4-6
1 medium ripe pineapple
450 ml (15 fl oz) double or whipping cream
75 g (3 oz) macaroons, roughly crushed
2 tablespoons Kirsch
angelica leaves, to decorate

Preparation time: 25 minutes, plus chilling

1. Remove the green top from the pineapple, cut it in half lengthways, reserving the better half for decoration. Cut away the skin from the pineapple, removing the 'eyes' with the point of a knife. Cut into slices, then cut each slice in half and blot dry. Remove the core if hard.
2. Whip the cream until 'floppy' and reserve one-third. Stir the macaroons into the remaining cream.
3. Sandwich the half slices of pineapple together with macaroon cream, to form a roll on a flat serving plate.
4. Stir the Kirsch into the reserved cream and use to mask the pineapple completely. Mark the cream to simulate pineapple skin and decorate with angelica leaves. Replace the green top. Chill until required.

SCOTTISH HONEY POSSETT

Serves 4-6
3 tablespoons medium oatmeal
6 tablespoons clear honey
grated rind and juice of ½ orange
2 tablespoons whisky
1 x 300 ml (10 fl oz) carton double or whipping cream
slices of orange, to decorate

Preparation time: 10 minutes, plus chilling

1. Spread the oatmeal evenly on a baking sheet and toast under a preheated medium hot grill for 2-3 minutes until golden brown. Allow to cool.
2. Place the honey, orange rind and juice, whisky and cream in a bowl. Whisk until 'floppy', about 3-5 minutes with an electric whisk.
3. Stir in the oatmeal and spoon into individual glasses. Decorate with orange slices.

FROM THE LEFT: Pineapple and kirsch roll; Rhubarb mallow; Scandinavian raspberry flummery

RHUBARB MALLOW

Serves 4-6

1 x 525 g (1 lb 3 oz) can rhubarb
1 lemon jelly tablet
few drops edible red food colouring (optional)
1 egg white
12 marshmallows, chopped with wetted scissors
julienne strips of lemon rind, to decorate (optional)

Preparation time: 15 minutes, plus chilling
Cooking time: about 5 minutes to dissolve jelly

1. Drain the juice from the rhubarb into a saucepan and dissolve the jelly tablet in it over gentle heat.
2. Purée the rhubarb in a liquidizer. Transfer the purée to a bowl. Add the dissolved jelly and add a few drops of red colouring if preferred. Chill until on the point of setting.
3. Whisk the egg white until stiff. Fold the egg white and marshmallows into the jelly. Transfer to a serving dish and chill until set.
4. Cut fine julienne strips of lemon. Decorate the top of the rhubarb mallow with the lemon rind (if using).

SCANDINAVIAN RASPBERRY FLUMMERY

Serves 6

450 g (1 lb) raspberries, hulled
300 ml (½ pint) water
175 g (6 oz) caster sugar
50 g (2 oz) semolina

Preparation time: 10 minutes
Cooking time: 20 minutes

1. Reserve 12 raspberries for decoration. Place the remainder in a saucepan with the water and 50 g (2 oz) of the sugar. Simmer for 5 mintues until very soft. Sieve to remove the seeds and make up to 600 ml (1 pint) with water.
2. Return the raspberry purée to the cleaned saucepan. Bring to the boil, stir in the remaining sugar and the semolina and simmer for 10 minutes, stirring frequently.
3. Turn the mixture into a large bowl and whisk with an electric whisk for about 5 minutes until light and fluffy. Serve warm in individual dishes. Decorate with the reserved raspberries and serve with single cream.

BUTTERSCOTCH MOUSSE

Serves 6
600 ml (1 pint) milk
40 g (1½ oz) cornflour
175 g (6 oz) demerara sugar
50 g (2 oz) butter
1 teaspoon vanilla essence
2 egg whites
To decorate:
whipped cream
chocolate 'coffee beans'

Chocolate 'coffee beans' can be bought from confectioners and delicatessens.

Preparation time: 15 minutes, plus chilling

1. Blend a little of the milk with the cornflour to a smooth paste. Add the remaining milk and cook, stirring, over gentle heat until thickened. Simmer for 1 minute.
2. Dissolve the sugar in a pan over medium heat until completely liquid. Remove from the heat, cool slightly, then stir in the butter until melted.
3. Working quickly, stir the sugar mixture into the white sauce, mixing until smooth. Strain and cool slightly. Stir in the vanilla essence.
4. Whisk the egg whites until stiff and fold into the sauce. Pour into a serving dish and chill for several hours.
5. Just before serving, decorate with whipped cream and chocolate coffee beans.

CHOCOLATE CURLS
The Easy way Take small pieces of chocolate and scrape curls off with a potato peeler. Chocolate cake covering is often easier to use for this method.
The Professional way Spread melted chocolate on a cool dry surface; marble is the best, but a formica chopping board will do. Keep the surface of the chocolate as smooth as possible. Leave the chocolate to set. Using a large sharp kitchen knife held at a 45° angle, push the knife away from yourself along the chocolate. The chocolate will roll and form curls at the edge of the knife.

SPICED MUSCOVADO SWIRL

Serves 8
1 x 300 ml (10 fl oz) carton double or whipping cream
450 g (1 lb) plain unsweetened yogurt
grated rind of 1 lemon
100 g (4 oz) Muscovado (raw cane) sugar
2 teaspoons mixed spice

Preparation time: 8 minutes, plus chilling

1. Whip the cream, then stir in the yogurt and lemon rind. Spoon into a serving dish or 8 individual dishes.
2. Mix the Muscovado sugar and spice and sprinkle in a thick layer over the mixture.
3. Chill for at least 2 hours until the sugar is completely moist. Just before serving, carefully swirl the sugar through the mixture. Serve with thin crisp biscuits.

FROM THE LEFT: Spiced muscovado swirl; Chestnut creams; Honeycomb fool

CHESTNUT CREAMS

1 x 150 ml (5 fl oz) carton double or whipping cream
2 tablespoons rum or brandy
1 x 225 g (8 oz) can sweetened chestnut spread
chocolate curls, to decorate

Preparation time: 10 minutes, plus chilling

1. Whip the cream and rum or brandy together until just 'floppy'.
2. Gradually fold in the chestnut spread. Spoon the mixture into a piping bag fitted with a large star nozzle.
3. Pipe into small individual glasses. Chill until required.
4. Decorate each dessert with chocolate curls, and if preferred serve with single cream.

HONEYCOMB FOOL

1 egg white
250 ml (8 fl oz) double or whipping cream
4 milk chocolate honeycomb bars
twists of orange rind to decorate

Preparation time: 10 minutes, plus chilling

1. Place the honeycomb bars in a strong plastic bag. Hold the open end of the bag securely and crush into rough pieces with a rolling pin.
2. Whisk the egg white until stiff, then whip the cream until stiff. Fold the egg white into the cream.
3. Stir in the crushed honeycomb bars.
4. Spoon the mixture into individual dishes.
5. Chill until required, then decorate with twists of orange rind.

CHOUX FRITTERS WITH STRAWBERRY AND REDCURRANT SAUCE

Serves 6
50 g (2 oz) butter
150 ml (¼ pint) water
65 g (2½ oz) plain flour, sifted
25 g (1 oz) caster sugar
2 eggs, beaten
oil for deep frying
icing sugar
Sauce:
50 g (2 oz) granulated sugar
300 ml (½ pint) water
2 teaspoons cornflour
2 tablespoons brandy
100 g (4 oz) redcurrants, stems removed
225 g (8 oz) strawberries, roughly chopped

Preparation time: 15 minutes
Cooking time: about 25 minutes

1. To make the choux paste, place the butter and water in a saucepan. Heat until the butter melts, then bring to the boil. Off the heat, immediately add the flour and sugar and beat well to a thick paste.
2. Allow to cool slightly, then beat in the egg, a little at a time, until the mixture is smooth. Spoon the choux paste into a piping bag fitted with a large star nozzle. Chill until required.
3. For the sauce, place the sugar and water in a saucepan and heat gently until the sugar dissolves. Boil rapidly for 2 minutes.
4. Mix the cornflour, brandy and lemon juice to a smooth paste. Add to the sugar syrup and bring to the boil, stirring. Add the fruit and simmer for 5 minutes.
5. Heat the oil for deep frying to 182°C (360°F), or until a cube of bread rises instantly to the surface. Pipe 4 cm (1½ inch) lengths of choux paste into the oil. Cut each length free with a wetted knife. Fry in 3 or 4 batches, for 2-3 minutes until golden and puffy. Drain on kitchen paper.
6. Sprinkle with icing sugar and serve at once with the strawberry and redcurrant sauce.

LAYERED CHOCOLATE CRUNCH

Serves 6
100 g (4 oz) wholemeal breadcrumbs
100 g (4 oz) demerara sugar
6 tablespoons drinking chocolate
2 teaspoons instant coffee powder
1 x 150 ml (5 fl oz) carton single cream
1 x 150 ml (5 fl oz) carton double or whipping cream
6 tablespoons black cherry or strawberry jam
chocolate lacework (page 46), to decorate

Preparation time: 15 minutes, plus chilling

This is a very simple desert which combines several layers, producing a contrast of tastes and textures.

1. In a mixing bowl combine the breadcrumbs, sugar, chocolate and coffee powder.
2. Whip the creams together until the whisk makes a trail in the cream but it is still 'runny'.
3. Spoon 1 tablespoon of jam into each of 6 individual dishes, then arrange layers of cream and breadcrumb mixture, finishing with a layer of breadcrumb mixture and a spoonful of cream. Chill for several hours.
4. Just before serving decorate with chocolate lacework.

APRICOT TOASTS

1 egg
1 tablespoon milk
4 small slices fruit or plain bread, crusts removed
40 g (1½ oz) butter
2 tablespoons caster sugar
½ teaspoon ground cinnamon
1 x 275 g (10 oz) can apricot halves in juice, drained
whipped cream
1 tablespoon chopped pistachios or toasted almonds

Preparation time: 5 minutes
Cooking time: 5 minutes

Bread, whether sweet or plain, dipped in a custard mixture and pan fried is known in France as Pain Perdu and England as Poor Knights of Windsor. In both countries the recipe dates back to Medieval times. The dessert can be simply served sprinkled with sugar and topped with jam or cream or more sumptuously with brandied fruits. For a richer custard substitute cream for the milk.

SUGARED CHOCOLATE PANCAKES

50 g (2 oz) plain flour
pinch of salt
3 tablespoons caster sugar
2-3 tablespoons oil
2 eggs, separated
6 tablespoons milk
50 g (2 oz) plain chocolate, grated
large knob of butter

Preparation time: 15 minutes
Cooking time: 15-20 minutes

1. Sift the flour, salt and 2 tablespoons of the sugar into a mixing bowl. Add 1 tablespoon of the oil, the egg yolks and milk and beat to a smooth batter.
2. Whisk the egg whites to soft peaks and fold into the batter.
3. Use the batter to make 8 small pancakes (page 54) and fry in the remaining oil, but cook only on one side.
4. Sprinkle some chocolate on the uncooked side of each pancake and roll up. Place in a generously buttered ovenproof dish and sprinkle with the remaining sugar. Place under a preheated grill for 5-10 minutes to warm through. Serve at once.

1. Beat the egg and milk together and dip the bread slices in it until coated on both sides.
2. Melt the butter and fry the slices of bread until crisp and golden on both sides. Drain on absorbent kitchen paper.
3. Mix the sugar and cinnamon together and sprinkle on to the bread. Top with apricots, a whirl of whipped cream and chopped nuts. Serve at once.

CLOCKWISE FROM THE TOP: Choux fritters with strawberry and redcurrant sauce; Layered chocolate crunch; Apricot toasts

CHERRIES IN RED WINE

450 g (1 lb) red or black cherries, stoned
300 ml (½ pint) light red wine
4 tablespoons sugar
½ teaspoon ground cinnamon
2 teaspoons cornflour
4 tablespoons redcurrant jelly

Preparation time: 5 minutes
Cooking time: 5 minutes

1. Place the cherries, wine, sugar and cinnamon in a saucepan. Bring slowly to the boil.
2. Mix the cornflour and redcurrant jelly and stir into the wine. Simmer for 1 minute. Remove from the heat. Cover and leave for 5 minutes.
3. Serve warm or cold, preferably with vanilla ice cream. If a thicker sauce is desired, remove the cherries and reduce the liquid until it reaches the required consistency.

BANANA FLAMBÉ

6 medium bananas, peeled and cut in half lengthways
50 g (2 oz) butter, melted
50 g (2 oz) light brown sugar
4 tablespoons brandy
flaked almonds, toasted, to decorate

Preparation time: 7-8 minutes

1. Fry the bananas in the melted butter until golden and just tender.
2. Sprinkle in the sugar and stir carefully to coat the fruit. Stir in the brandy.
3. Bring to the boil. Immediately set alight and serve sprinkled with a few flaked almonds.

Variation:
For Peach Flambé, use 4-6 fresh peaches, halved and stoned, in place of the bananas.

BRANDIED PEACHES

4 large ripe peaches
lemon juice
2 tablespoons caster sugar
4 tablespoons brandy

Preparation time: 10 minutes, plus marinating

1. Dip the peaches in boiling water for about 20 seconds. Dip immediately in cold water and leave to go cold. Remove the skins and toss the fruit in lemon juice.
2. Prick the peaches with fork or skewer and place in a dish. Sprinkle with the sugar and brandy. Cover and chill for several hours until the flavours are absorbed. Serve with whipped cream.

CLOCKWISE FROM THE TOP: Brandied peaches; Cherries in red wine; Blackberry and apple compôte; Banana flambé

BLACKBERRY AND APPLE COMPÔTE

750 g (1½-1¾ lb) dessert apples, peeled and cored
squeeze of lemon juice
50 g (2 oz) sugar
300 ml (½ pint) water
225 g (8 oz) blackberries, prepared
2 tablespoons brandy

Preparation time: 10 minutes, plus chilling
Cooking time: 15 minutes

1. Thickly slice the apples and place in a large shallow pan with the lemon juice, sugar and water. Simmer gently until just tender, about 5-7 minutes.
2. Drain the apples, reserving the juice. Place the apple slices in a serving dish with the blackberries.
3. Boil the juice until slightly syrupy, then remove from the heat and stir in the brandy. Pour over the fruit and chill until cold.
4. Serve with ice cream or single cream.

Variation:

For Pear and Raspberry Compôte, substitute peeled cored and sliced pears and fresh raspberries. If preferred, use Kirsch instead of brandy. Prepare as recipe.

COLD DESSERTS

PASKHA

Serves 8-10
1 egg
50 g (2 oz) caster sugar
50 g (2 oz) unsalted butter, softened
450 g (1 lb) cream cheese
150 ml (5 fl oz) soured cream
50 g (2 oz) whole almonds, toasted and chopped
50 g (2 oz) raisins
50 g (2 oz) cut mixed peel
50 g (2 oz) multi-coloured glacé cherries, quartered
½ teaspoon rosewater
crystallized fruits, to decorate

Preparation time: 20 minutes, plus overnight draining

Paskha literally translated means Easter and this dessert takes its name from the Russian Easter. It is traditionally made with curd cheese (so if you want a sharper, less creamier taste, you may like to try it) and is pressed into a wooden, pyramid-shaped mould, turned out and decorated with crystallized fruit.

1. Whisk the egg and sugar until pale and thick. Beat in the butter and cream cheese, then the soured cream.
2. Fold in the remaining ingredients.
3. Line a 1.2 litre (2 pint) thoroughly cleaned terra cotta flower pot with muslin or a fine teatowel. Spoon the mixture into the pot and fold in the edges of the muslin.
4. Place a saucer on top of the mixture and add a 1 kg (2 lb) weight. Place the flowerpot on a cooling tray set over a large plate.
5. Chill in the refrigerator for 24 hours, allowing any moisture to drain into the plate.
6. Unmould, smooth the surface with a palette knife and decorate with crystallized fruit, cut into different shapes and arranged on the top and sides in a pattern of your choice.

BAKED SULTANA CHEESECAKE ✓

Serves 8
450 g (1 lb) cream cheese
1 x 150 ml (5 fl oz) carton double cream
75 g (3 oz) caster sugar
grated rind of 1 lemon
1 tablespoon lemon juice
40 g (1½ oz) cornflour
2 eggs
50 g (2 oz) sultanas
100 g (4 oz) shortcrust pastry
icing sugar, to decorate.

Preparation time: 15 minutes
Cooking time: 55 minutes
Oven: 190°C, 375°F, Gas Mark 5;
180°C, 350°F, Gas Mark 4

1. Beat together the cream cheese, cream, sugar, lemon rind and juice, and eggs until smooth. Toss the sultanas in the cornflour and add them to the mixture. Beat until the ingredients are thoroughly combined.
2. Roll out the pastry and use to bottom-line a 20 cm (8 inch) spring form tin. Prick the pastry with a fork and bake in a preheated oven for 20 minutes. Reduce the heat.
3. Pour the cheese mixture over the pastry and return to the oven at the lower temperature for 35 minutes. Switch off the oven but leave the cheesecake in it until cold. Chill until required.
4. Unmould on to a serving plate. Dust the surface with icing sugar and mark with a lattice pattern using the back of a long-bladed knife.

Variation:
Try peach or apricot cheesecake; sprinkle 100 g (4 oz) well drained, and chopped canned peaches or apricots over the baked pastry base. Omit the sultanas from the mixture and continue as per recipe.

ABOVE: Paskha; BELOW: Baked sultana cheesecake

CARAMEL CREAM WITH STRAWBERRIES

Serves 6
900 ml (1½ pints) milk
4 eggs
4 egg yolks
4 tablespoons caster sugar
grated rind of 1 small orange
450 g (1 lb) strawberries, to decorate
Caramel:
175 g (6 oz) caster sugar
12 tablespoons water

Preparation time: 20 minutes, plus cooling
Cooking time: 1½ hours
Oven: 170°C, 325°F, Gas Mark 3

1. Warm the milk. Beat the eggs, egg yolks and sugar together, then pour the warm milk on top and mix well. Strain through a fine sieve, then stir in the orange rind.
2. Dissolve the sugar in the water over a gentle heat, bring to the boil and boil to a rich caramel colour. Pour the caramel into a buttered 20 cm (8 inch) – 1.5 litre (2½ pint) – soufflé dish, swirling it round to cover the sides. Allow to cool.
3. Pour in the egg custard mixture and place the soufflé dish in a water bath (a roasting tin with water to come at least halfway up the sides of the dish). Make sure the water is boiling. Cover the soufflé dish with foil.
4. Bake in a preheated oven for 1 hour 15 minutes. Leave until cold, then refrigerate until required.
5. Unmould on to a flat serving dish and decorate with strawberries.

Variation:
If preferred, serve the caramel cream with orange segments. To do this, take 3 oranges. Using a sharp knife, cut the peel and bitter white pith from each orange. To free the segments, cut between the flesh and membrane at either side. Remove all the segments and squeeze the remains of the orange to extract all the juice.

> To check if a baked custard such as Caramel Cream is cooked, make a small incision in the top of the custard with the point of a knife. The knife should come out clean. After cooking, always remove the custard from the water bath and leave until completely cold and preferably chilled before unmoulding.

FROMAGE À LA CRÈME

Serves 6
225 g (8 oz) cottage cheese, sieved
3 egg whites
4 tablespoons caster sugar
6 tablespoons double cream
fresh strawberries or cherries, to decorate

Preparation time: 15 minutes, plus overnight draining

1. Place the cheese in a basin and beat until smooth.
2. Whisk the egg whites until stiff and whisk in half the sugar, a tablespoon at a time. Fold into the cheese.
3. Press the mixture into 6 muslin-lined coeur à la crème dishes. Cover and leave to drain in the refrigerator overnight.
4. Turn out on to individual plates, and decorate with fruit. Just before serving, spoon a tablespoon of cream and a teaspoon of caster sugar over each 'heart'.

FROM THE LEFT: Caramel cream with strawberries; Fromage à la crème

CRÈME BRÛLÉE
(OLD ENGLISH BURNT CREAM)

1 x 300 ml (10 fl oz) carton double cream
1 bay leaf
4 egg yolks
25 g (1 oz) plus 4-6 tablespoons caster sugar
1 teaspoon cornflour

Preparation time: 30 minutes, plus chilling
Cooking time: 25-30 minutes

Crème Brûlée is a very rich smooth custard topped with a hard caramel glaze.

1. Warm the cream and bay leaf to just below boiling point.
2. Whisk the egg yolks with 25 g (1 oz) sugar and the cornflour until pale and thick. Stir in the cream and place in a basin over a saucepan of hot water. Cook, stirring frequently, until the mixture is thick enough to coat the back of a wooden spoon, about 25 minutes.
3. Strain into 4 small ramekin dishes. Chill for several hours.
4. Spread a layer of caster sugar over the top of each ramekin dish, making sure the custard is completely covered.
5. Place the dishes under the preheated grill until the sugar melts to a golden caramel. Chill again for several hours.
6. The caramel may be cracked with a teaspoon before serving.

LEMON WINE SYLLABUB

Serves 4-6

150 ml (¼ pint) white wine or sherry
75 g (3 oz) caster sugar
2 tablespoons lemon juice
2 teaspoons grated lemon rind
1 x 300 ml (10 fl oz) carton double or whipping cream
julienne strips of lemon rind, to decorate

Preparation time: 10 minutes, plus marinating

This dish should be eaten the day it is prepared, other-wise it will separate.

1. Place the wine, sugar, lemon juice and rind in a basin. Leave to infuse for 1 hour.
2. Add the cream and whisk the mixture until it is stiff enough to stand in soft peaks, about 5 minutes with an electric hand whisk.
3. Spoon into individual glasses and decorate with lemon rind. Chill until required.

BLACKCURRANT WHIP

Serves 6

450 g (1 lb) blackcurrants
100 g (4 oz) sugar
1 tablespoon gelatine
3 tablespoons water
2 tablespoons Crème de Cassis or Kirsch
3 egg whites
1 x 150 ml (5 fl oz) carton double or whipping cream
whipped cream, to decorate (optional)

Preparation time: 25 minutes
Cooking time: 10 minutes

1. Place the blackcurrants and sugar in a saucepan and simmer gently until the fruit is soft. Reserve 6 teaspoons blackcurrants for decoration. Purée the remainder and sieve to remove the pips. Cool.
2. Dissolve the gelatine in the water and stir into the blackcurrant purée. Stir in the Crème de Cassis or Kirsch.
3. Whisk the egg whites until stiff and whip the cream until it stands in soft peaks. Fold the cream and then the egg whites into the cold blackcurrant purée.
4. Spoon into individual dishes and chill until set.
5. Decorate each with a teaspoon of blackcurrants and whipped cream (if using).

ABOVE: Lemon wine syllabub; BELOW Blackcurrant whip

GOOSEBERRY FOOL

225 g (8 oz) gooseberries, topped and tailed
1 tablespoon water
75 g (3 oz) caster sugar
1 egg white
1 x 150 ml (5 fl oz) carton double or whipping cream, whipped
    until stiff

Preparation time: 15 minutes, plus chilling
Cooking time: 10 minutes

1. Simmer the gooseberries in the water for about 10 minutes until soft. Leave to cool, then purée and sieve to remove the seeds. Stir in 50 g (2 oz) of the sugar and chill until very cold.
2. Whisk the egg white until stiff, then whisk in the remaining sugar until glossy. Fold in the whipped cream.
3. Fold the gooseberry purée into the cream mixture and spoon into individual glasses. Chill until required. If preferred, spoon a few stewed gooseberries into the bottom of the glasses before adding the fool.

Variation:

For Mango fool, peel a large ripe mango and remove the flesh. Purée, then stir in 25 g (1 oz) caster sugar and 1 teaspoon of lime or lemon juice. Continue as for gooseberry fool.

If preferred, put chopped mango into the bottom of the glasses before spooning in the fool.

Use this recipe as a basic guide line for almost any fruit fool of your choice. Continue as above for berry fruits such as fresh blackcurrants, blackberries, etc which need cooking before puréeing. Other soft fruits, for example raspberries, strawberries, simply need puréeing (as mango) and sieving to remove any seeds. You need about 150 ml (¼ pint) prepared purée sweetened to taste.

As an alternative decoration use some of the fresh or stewed fruit on top of the fool.

ABOVE: Gooseberry fool, BELOW: Mango fool

BLACK CHERRY AND CREAM CHEESE STRUDEL

Serves 8
225 g (8 oz) plain flour
pinch of salt
1 egg
2 tablespoons oil
2-3 tablespoons lukewarm water
Filling:
50 g (2 oz) butter, melted
6 tablespoons ground almonds
450 g (1 lb) cream cheese
50 g (2 oz) sugar
1 teaspoon ground cinnamon
2 egg yolks
1 x 425 g (15 oz) can pitted black cherries, drained
1 tablespoon icing sugar

Preparation time: 25 minutes, plus resting
Cooking time: 30 minutes
Oven: 200°C, 400°F, Gas Mark 6

1. Sift the flour and salt into a mixing bowl. Beat together the remaining pastry ingredients and mix into the flour to give a soft dough. Cover and leave to rest for 1 hour.
2. Lightly knead the pastry on a floured surface, then roll out as thinly as possible on a floured tea towel to approx 50 x 63 cm (20 x 25 inches), or until you can see your hand clearly through the pastry.
3. Brush with melted butter and sprinkle with ground almonds.
4. Beat the cream cheese, sugar, cinnamon and egg yolks together. Stir in the cherries. Spread this mixture over the pastry to within 4 cm (1½ inches) of the edges.
5. Roll up carefully from a long edge. Fold in the ends. Place on a lightly greased baking sheet and bake for about 30 minutes until golden. Cool and sprinkle with icing sugar. Serve just warm.

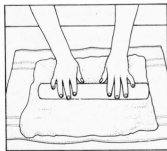

On a floured tea towel roll out the pastry as thinly as possible, using long firm strokes.

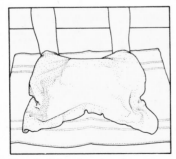

Place both hands, palms down underneath the pastry. Gently move your hands apart to stretch the pastry further.

FLOATING ISLANDS

Serves 4-6
2 egg whites
100 g (4 oz) caster sugar
600 ml (1 pint) milk
2 tablespoons caster sugar
3 eggs
1 tablespoon cornflour
few drops of vanilla essence
To decorate:
25 g (1 oz) whole almonds
25 g (1 oz) caster sugar

Preparation time: 30 minutes
Cooking time: 25 minutes

1. Whisk the egg whites until stiff. Whisk in the sugar, a tablespoonful at a time, until thick and glossy
2. Heat the milk and sugar to simmering point. Slide 4 separate tablespoons of egg white mixture into the milk. Simmer for 3 minutes. Drain on a clean teatowel. Repeat twice to make 12 meringue 'islands'.
3. Beat together the eggs and cornflour, stir in the hot milk and vanilla essence. Strain into a clean saucepan and cook gently, stirring all the time, until thick enough to coat the back of a wooden spoon. Cool and pour into a serving dish.
4. Place the whole almonds and sugar in a saucepan. Heat gently without stirring until the sugar turns caramel coloured. Pour on to a buttered baking sheet and leave until cold. Chop fairly finely when set.
5. Place the meringue 'islands' on the egg custard. Sprinkle with the almond caramel and serve at once.

To shape the 'islands', take up a portion of the meringue mixture on 1 tablespoon.

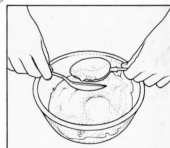

Using a second tablespoon, pass the meringue between the two until a smooth egg shape is formed.

WHITE CHOCOLATE MOUSSE

Serves 5-6

150 g (5 oz) white chocolate, broken into pieces
1½ tablespoons cornflour
2 tablespoons water
2 tablespoons light rum
3 egg whites
50 g (2 oz) caster sugar
kiwi fruit slices, to decorate

Preparation time: 15 minutes, plus chilling
Cooking time: 2-3 minutes

1. Place the chocolate pieces in a saucepan.
2. Blend the cornflour and water and add to the pan. Cook over gentle heat, stirring until the chcolate is melted and the sauce thickened. Chill until cold.
3. Beat in the rum. Whisk the egg whites until stiff and whisk in the sugar, a tablespoon at a time. Fold a little of the egg white mixture into the chocolate, then return this to the egg white and fold in carefully.
4. Spoon into individual dishes and chill until firm. Decorate with kiwi fruit slices.

Variation:
For Dark Chocolate Mousse, use plain chocolate and dark rum. Omit the cornflour. Proceed as above. Decorate with orange segments (page 24) or strawberries.

PEAR AND ORANGE BRISTOL

Serves 4-6
6 small pears, peeled, cored and quartered
200 ml (⅓ pint) water
175 g (6 oz) sugar
2 large oranges

Preparation time: 35 minutes, plus cooling
Cooking time: 15 minutes

1. Place the pear quarters in a large shallow pan with the water and half the sugar. Simmer gently until the fruit is tender, about 10 minutes. Drain and reserve the syrup.
2. Pare the rind from 1 orange and cut into julienne strips. Place the strips in a pan with a little water and bring to the boil. Rinse in cold water and drain.
3. Cut away the white pith from the orange. Peel the other orange. Slice both fruits thinly.
4. Place the remaining sugar in a saucepan over medium heat and cook without stirring, until light caramel in colour. Pour immediately on to an oiled baking sheet. Allow to set, then break into chips.
5. Place the oranges and pears in a serving dish. Pour the syrup over and chill until required.
6. Just before serving, sprinkle with orange strips and caramel chips.

Variation:
Serves 6: To make caramelized tangerines, prepare caramel chips as above. Pare the rind and pith from 12 firm skinned tangerines. Place half the sugar and the water in a small saucepan and heat gently until the sugar has dissolved. Simmer the syrup over a medium heat for 5 minutes. Allow to cool. Place the tangerines in a serving dish and pour over the cooled syrup. Sprinkle with three-quarters of the caramel chips and chill for 2-3 hours. Add the remaining caramel chips just before serving.

TANGY LIME MOUSSE

Serves 8
25 g (1 oz) cornflour
450 ml (¾ pint) milk
100 g (4 oz) caster sugar
3 eggs, separated
grated rind and juice of 4 limes
15 g (½ oz) gelatine
few drops of edible green food colouring
To decorate:
fresh lime slices
whipped cream (optional)

Preparation time: 15 minutes
Cooking time: 5 minutes

1. Mix the cornflour with a little of the milk. Beat in the sugar and egg yolks.
2. Heat the rest of the milk and stir into the mixture. Return to the pan and cook, stirring, until the mixture is thickened. Off the heat, stir in the grated lime rind.
3. Dissolve the gelatine in the lime juice over gentle heat and stir into the custard. Add 1-2 drops edible green food colouring.
4. Whisk the egg whites until stiff and fold into the mixture. Spoon into a serving dish and chill until firm.
5. Decorate with lime slices and/or whipped cream.

PEPPERMINT PEARS

100 g (4 oz) sugar
300 ml (½ pint) water
1 tablespoon lemon juice
8 small conference pears
3 tablespoons Crème de Menthe
few drops edible green food colouring
sprigs of mint, to decorate

Preparation time: 20 minutes, plus chilling
Cooking time: about 35 minutes

RED FRUIT SALAD

Serves 6-8
100 g (4 oz) sugar
300 ml (½ pint) water
rind and juice of ½ lemon
1 kg (2 lb) mixed red fruits, such as redcurrants, raspberries, strawberries, cherries and plums

Preparation time: 30 minutes
Cooking time: 15 minutes

1. Place the sugar and water in a saucepan with the pared lemon rind. Heat gently to dissolve the sugar, then bring to the boil and boil gently for 10 minutes. Cool, then remove the lemon rind. Stir in the lemon juice.
2. Prepare the fruit as necessary – top and tail redcurrants, hull raspberries and strawberries, and slice or halve strawberries, stone cherries and plums. Cut plums into slices.
3. Place the prepared fruit in a dish, cover with lemon syrup and chill until required.

Variation:
Use 'green' fruits instead of red, i.e. melon, grapes, pears, apples, bananas, kiwi fruits, greengages. Make melon balls, peel and seed grapes, peel and slice pears, apples, bananas and kiwi fruits.

1. Place the sugar, water and lemon juice in a saucepan over gentle heat until the sugar dissolves.
2. Peel the pears, leaving the stalks intact. Cut a slice from the base of each pear so that they can stand up. Using a small pointed knife, carefully scoop out the pips, starting from the base so that the pears remain whole.
3. Add the Crème de Menthe and green colouring to the sugar syrup and bring to the boil. Place the pears, standing upright, in the saucepan. Cover and simmer for 20-25 minutes until tender.
4. Remove the pears to a serving dish. Boil the syrup rapidly until fairly thick, then spoon over the pears. Chill for several hours, spooning the syrup over them from time to time. Decorate with sprigs of mint.

FROM THE TOP: Peppermint pears;
Green fruit salad (variation); Tangy lime mousse

FESTIVE FLAN

Serves 8-10
175 g (6 oz) plain flour, sifted
100 g (4 oz) butter
25 g (1 oz) caster sugar
1 egg yolk
1 tablespoon cold water
Filling:
350 g (12 oz) mincemeat
1 dessert apple, peeled, cored and diced
1 banana, peeled and diced
2 tablespoons brandy
1 x ½ litre (17½ fl oz) carton vanilla ice cream

Preparation time: 30 minutes, plus chilling
Cooking time: 40 minutes
Oven: 200°C, 400°F, Gas Mark 6

1. Place the flour in a mixing bowl. Rub in the butter. Stir in the sugar and egg yolk and add sufficient water to bind the mixture and produce a firm dough.
2. Roll out on a lightly floured surface and use to line a 24 cm (9½ inch) flan dish or tin. Chill, then bake 'blind' for 25-30 minutes until completely baked and golden. Leave until cold.
3. Meanwhile, place the mincemeat, apple, banana and brandy in a saucepan. Cover and simmer gently for 10 minutes. Allow to cool.
4. Fill the flan case with scoops of ice cream, spoon over the mincemeat mixture and serve at once.

Variation:
Raspberry ripple flan: Make the flan case as above, then use raspberry ripple ice cream and a prepared fresh raspberry sauce. To make the sauce, place 350 g (12 oz) fresh or frozen raspberries in a saucepan, add 75 g (3 oz) sugar and 1 teaspoon arrowroot powder. Stir frequently, over a gentle heat, until the sauce just comes to the boil and thickens. Allow to cool. Stir in 1 tablespoon Cointreau or Grand Marnier. Fill the flan case with scoops of raspberry ripple ice cream. If preferred, decorate with 2 fresh peaches, skinned, stoned and thinly sliced. Pour over the raspberry sauce and serve immediately.

APPLE MINCEMEAT JALOUSIE

Serves 4-6
350 g (12 oz) cooking apples, peeled, cored and chopped
1 tablespoon water
225 g (8 oz) mincemeat
350 g (12 oz) frozen puff pastry, thawed
beaten egg, to glaze
3 tablespoons golden syrup or honey

Preparation time: 20 minutes
Cooking time: 30-35 minutes
Oven: 220°C, 425°F, Gas Mark 7

1. Place the apples and water in a saucepan and simmer gently until the apples are just tender. Cool. Stir in the mincemeat.
2. Roll out the pastry on a lightly floured surface to an oblong 45 x 18 cm (18 x 7 inches). Cut into two 23 x 18 cm (9 x 7 inch) oblongs.
3. Place one oblong on a wetted baking sheet. Spoon the apples and mincemeat into the centre, leaving a 2 cm (¾ inch) edge of pastry. Moisten the edge of the pastry.
4. Fold the second oblong of pastry lightly in half lengthways and with a floured knife make cuts 1 cm (½ inch) apart to within 2 cm (¾ inch) of the edge. Open out the pastry and position over the first piece. Seal the edges well, knock up and flute. Brush with beaten egg.
5. Bake in a preheated oven for 20-25 minutes until crisp and golden. Brush with golden syrup or honey whilst still warm. Cool on a wire tray.

Variation:
Cranberry, mincemeat and walnut jalousie
Omit the apples and simmer 175 g (6 oz) cranberries with 1 tablespoon water and 25 g (1 oz) sugar, until they start to pop, about 5 minutes. Cool and stir in the mincemeat and 50 g (2 oz) chopped walnuts. Continue as recipe.

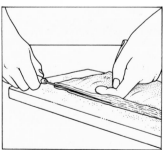 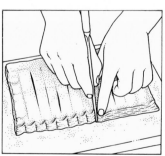

To 'knock up' the pastry, use the back of a knife to make a series of shallow horizontal cuts in the sealed pastry edge.

Holding the knife vertically, with your index finger as a guide, indent the pastry at regular intervals to give a fluted edge.

FROM THE LEFT: Apple mincemeat jalousie; Golden syrup tart

GOLDEN SYRUP TART

Serves 8

350 g (12 oz) shortcrust pastry
350 g (12 oz) golden syrup
50 g (2 oz) ground almonds
grated rind and juice of ½ small lemon
1 egg
6 tablespoons double cream
75 g (3 oz) fresh white breadcrumbs

Preparation time: 15 minutes
Cooking time: 30 minutes
Oven: 190°C, 375°F, Gas Mark 5

1. Roll out the pastry and use to line a 25 cm (10 inch) French fluted flan tin. Prick the base with a fork, then chill until required.
2. Combine all the remaining ingredients and pour into the prepared case. Bake in a preheated oven for about 30 minutes until just set.

Variation:
If wished use the pastry trimmings to make a lattice. To do this, re-roll the trimmings and cut 8 strips about 1 cm (½ inch) wide and the length of the diameter of the flan. Arrange the strips in a lattice pattern. Wet the ends of the strips and press them firmly to the edge of the pastry case.

RASPBERRY SOUFFLÉ

Serves 4-6
3 eggs, separated
100 g (4 oz) caster sugar
450 g (1 lb) raspberries, puréed and sieved
15 g (½ oz) gelatine
2 tablespoons water
1 tablespoon lemon juice
1 x 150 ml (5 fl oz) carton double or whipping cream
To decorate:
whipped cream
fresh raspberries
angelica leaves

Preparation time: 40 minutes, plus chilling
Cooking time: 2 minutes

1. Cut a double thickness of greaseproof paper or foil, large enough to stand 5 cm (2 inches) above a 15 cm (6 inch) – 750 ml (1¼ pint) – soufflé dish and to wrap around it to make a collar. Lightly oil the section on the inside above the dish. Secure with paper clips or sticky tape. Place on a small baking sheet.
2. Whisk the egg yolks and sugar until pale and thick. Stir in the raspberry purée.
3. Dissolve the gelatine in the water and lemon juice (over heat) and stir into the raspberry mixture. Chill until just on the point of setting.
4. Whip the cream until it stands in soft peaks. Whisk the egg whites until stiff. Fold the cream and then the egg whites into the raspberry mixture. Spoon into the prepared dish. Chill for several hours until set.
5. Carefully remove the collar and decorate the dessert with rosettes of whipped cream, raspberries and angelica leaves.

Variation:
For Blackberry Soufflé, use blackberries instead of raspberries. Continue as above.

Secure the paper collar top and bottom with paper clips.

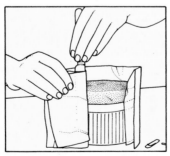

Gently remove the collar easing away with the help of a knife.

HAZELNUT CHEESECAKE

Serves 8-10
225 g (8 oz) digestive biscuits, crushed
100 g (4 oz) butter, melted
225 g (8 oz) cream cheese
100 g (4 oz) caster sugar
300 ml (10 fl oz) carton double or whipping cream
2 x 150 ml (5 fl oz) cartons hazelnut yogurt
50 g (2 oz) hazelnuts, roasted and roughly chopped, to decorate

Preparation time: 15 minutes, plus chilling

1. Mix the biscuit crumbs and butter and press on to the base of a 23 cm (9 inch) spring form tin. Chill.
2. Beat together the cream cheese and sugar until smooth. Whip the cream and fold into the cheese mixture. Finally, stir in the yogurt.
3. Spoon the cheese mixture on to the biscuit base and level the surface. Chill for several hours, then unmould and decorate the top with a layer of chopped roasted hazelnuts.

INDIVIDUAL LOGANBERRY SHORTBREAD

150 g (5 oz) plain flour
25 g (1 oz) ground rice
100 g (4 oz) butter, softened
50 g (2 oz) caster sugar
1 x 150 ml (5 fl oz) carton whipping cream
1 x 425 g (15 oz) can loganberries, drained, or 225 g (½ lb) fresh loganberries

Preparation time: 20 minutes
Cooking time: about 30 minutes
Oven: 170°C, 325°F, Gas Mark 3

1. Sift the flour and ground rice into a mixing bowl. Work in the butter and then the sugar with your fingertips to give a firm dough.
2. Roll out on a lightly floured surface to make four 10 cm (4 in) rounds. Place on a baking sheet. Flute the edges and prick with a fork.
3. Bake in a preheated oven for about 30 minutes until golden and firm. Leave until cold.
4. Whip the cream and spoon or pipe on to the shortbread rounds. Top with loganberries and serve at once.

CLOCKWISE FROM THE TOP: Hazelnut cheesecake;
Raspberry soufflé; Individual loganberry shortbread

GLAZED LEMON FLAN

Serves 8
175 g (6 oz) plain flour
pinch salt
75 g (3 oz) caster sugar
75 g (3 oz) butter, softened
3 egg yolks
Filling:
3 eggs
175 g (6 oz) caster sugar
grated rind and juice of 3 thin-skinned lemons
50 g (2 oz) butter, melted
Decoration:
50 g (2 oz) sugar
300 ml (½ pint) water
1 thin-skinned lemon, sliced

Preparation time: 30 minutes
Cooking time: 45 minutes
Oven: 190°C, 375°F, Gas Mark 5

In this recipe, the soft sharp filling contrasts well with the crisp, sweet pastry base.

1. For the pastry, sift the flour and salt into a basin. Stir in the caster sugar. Make a well in the centre and add the butter and egg yolks. Work together to give a firm dough. Knead on a lightly floured surface, roll out and use to line a 24 cm (9½ inch) French fluted flan tin. Chill.
2. Beat together the ingredients for the filling.
3. Dissolve the sugar in the water. Bring to the boil and boil for 2 minutes. Add the lemon slices and continue to boil gently until the syrup has almost disappeared, taking care that the lemon slices stay whole. Leave on a plate to cool.
4. Bake the pastry case 'blind' for 15 minutes in a preheated oven. Pour in the filling and return to the oven for a further 20-25 minutes until the filling is just set.
5. Allow to cool slightly, then decorate with halved lemon slices, arranged around the edge of the flan. Leave until cold.

FRENCH APPLE TART

Serves 8
175 g (6 oz) plain flour
pinch of salt
100 g (4 oz) unsalted butter
25 g (1 oz) sugar
1 tablespoon cold water
Filling:
4 large firm dessert apples
4 tablespoons caster sugar
3 egg yolks
1 tablespoon cornflour
250 ml (8 fl oz) mixed double cream and milk
few drops of vanilla essence
large knob of butter

Preparation time: 30 minutes, plus chilling
Cooking time: 40-45 minutes
Oven: 200°C, 400°F, Gas Mark 6
   180°C, 350°F, Gas Mark 4

French Apple Tart is a classic. In this version, the apples are arranged in fan shapes on the custard filling, instead of the usual concentric ring pattern.

1. Sift the flour and salt into a mixing bowl. Rub in the butter until the mixture resembles fine crumbs. Add the sugar and enough water to mix to a firm dough.
2. Roll out the pastry on a lightly floured surface and use to line a 25 cm (10 inch) French fluted flan tin. Chill.
3. Peel, core and halve the apples, then slice almost through to give a fan effect. Arrange in the pastry case and sprinkle with 1 tablespoon sugar. Bake in a preheated oven for 20 minutes. Reduce the heat.
4. Mix together the remaining sugar, egg yolks and cornflour. Heat the cream and milk together and pour over the egg mixture, stirring all the time. Strain, add the vanilla essence then pour carefully into the pastry case.
5. Return the tart to the oven for about 20 minutes until the custard is set. Halfway through cooking, dot the apples with the butter. Serve warm or cold.

FRESH GRAPE TART

Serves 6
125 g (4½ oz) plain flour
pinch of salt
75 g (3 oz) unsalted butter
1½ tablespoons caster sugar
about 2 teaspoons cold water
225 g (8 oz) large green grapes
175 g (6 oz) large black grapes
2 tablespoons apricot jam, sieved
1 tablespoon sherry
whipped cream, to decorate (optional)

Preparation time: 25 minutes, plus chilling
Cooking time: 35-40 minutes
Oven: 200°C, 400°F, Gas Mark 6

1. Sift the flour and salt into a mixing bowl. Rub in the butter until the mixture resembles fine crumbs. Stir in the sugar and sufficient water to give a firm dough.
2. Roll out on a lightly floured surface and use to line a 19 cm (7½ inch) French fluted flan tin. Chill until firm.
3. Bake 'blind' for 20 minutes in a preheated oven.
4. Meanwhile, using a skewer or a clean hairpin, remove the pips from the grapes. Arrange the grapes in alternating circles in the pastry case and return to the oven for 15 minutes. Bring the apricot jam and sherry to the boil, then cool and use to glaze the grapes. If preferred, pipe the outside edge of the flan with whipped cream.

FROM THE LEFT: Fresh grape tart; Glazed lemon flan; French apple tart

SPECIAL OCCASIONS

STRAWBERRY GÂTEAU

Serves 8
3 eggs
75 g (3 oz) caster sugar
75 g (3 oz) plain flour, sifted
350 g (12 oz) strawberries, washed and hulled
1 x 300 ml (½ pint) carton double or whipping cream
2 tablespoons Amaretto liqueur
175 g (6 oz) redcurrant jelly
1 tablespoon water
175 g (6 oz) marzipan

Preparation time: 40 minutes
Cooking time: 20 minutes
Oven: 200°C, 400°F, Gas Mark 6

Layers of delicate sponge are combined with strawberries and cream to make a sumptuous gâteau.

1. Grease and bottom-line 3 x 20 cm (8 inch) sandwich tins. Grease and flour the tins, shaking off excess flour.
2. Whisk the eggs and sugar together over hot water for about 5 minutes, until pale and thick. Remove from the heat and continue whisking for a further 5 minutes.
3. Fold in the flour with a metal spoon, then transfer the mixture to the prepared tins. Level the surface and bake in a preheated oven for 10 minutes, until risen and firm to the touch. Cool on a wire tray.
4. Halve sufficient strawberries to cover one layer of sponge completely. Mash the remaining fruit with a fork.
5. Whip the cream until stiff and spoon half into a piping bag fitted with a star nozzle. Fold the crushed strawberries into the remaining cream.
6. Sprinkle the 2 plain layers of sponge with Amaretto and sandwich together with half the strawberry cream, top with the remaining strawberry cream and then place the third sponge layer covered with strawberries on top.
7. Warm the redcurrant jelly with the water until melted.
8. Using a piece of string, measure the circumference and height of the cake. Roll out the marzipan to the exact size. Brush with redcurrant jelly and carefully press on to the sides of the cake. Use the remaining redcurrant jelly to glaze the top of the cake. Chill.
9. Pipe a decorative border of cream around the edge of the cake. Chill until required.

STRAWBERRY MALAKOFF

Serves 10-12
225 g (8 oz) unsalted butter
175 g (6 oz) caster sugar
175 g (6 oz) ground almonds
1 teaspoon almond extract
450 ml (15 fl oz) double cream
450 g (1 lb) small strawberries, hulled
about 21 sponge fingers
100 ml (4 fl oz) orange or almond liqueur

Preparation time: 30 minutes

1. Cream the butter and sugar until light and fluffy. Beat in the ground almond extract.
2. Whip the cream until it stands in soft peaks. Fold into the almond mixture. Reserve 12 strawberries for decoration. Fold the rest into the mixture (if large cut in half).
3. Cut a circle of greaseproof paper to fit the base of a 1.8 litre (3 pint) charlotte tin or soufflé dish.
4. Dip the sponge fingers into the liqueur one at a time and place them sugar side out around the inside edge of the dish. Add any remaining liqueur to the mixture.
5. Spoon the strawberry and almond mixture into the centre, pressing down lightly. Cover and chill until required.
6. Invert the dish on to a serving plate and allow to stand at room temperature for about 10 minutes before removing the mould. Decorate with the reserved strawberries.

Variation:
As an alternative presentation, make a cartwheel of sponge fingers to fit the base of the mould. You will need approximately 20 extra sponge fingers. Cut the biscuits slightly to form the design and arrange them on top of the greaseproof paper in the mould. Soak the biscuits in liqueur and proceed as above.

The fruit and liqueur may be varied according to taste, for example fresh raspberries and Framboise, blackberries and Kirsch.

ABOVE: Strawberry malakoff; BELOW: Strawberry gâteau

BRANDY ALEXANDER PIE

Serves 8
175 g (6 oz) plain flour
pinch of salt
100 g (4 oz) unsalted butter
25 g (1 oz) sugar
1 tablespoon cold water
Filling:
15 g (½ oz) gelatine
120 ml (4 fl oz) water
3 eggs, separated
75 g (3 oz) caster sugar
large pinch of salt
large pinch of nutmeg
50 ml (2 fl oz) brandy
50 ml (2 fl oz) Crème de cacao
250 ml (8 fl oz) double or whipping cream
To decorate:
whipped cream
chocolate curls (page 16)

Preparation time: 25-30 minutes
Cooking time: 25-30 minutes
Oven: 200°C, 400°F, Gas Mark 6

1. Sift the flour and salt into a mixing bowl. Rub in the butter, until the mixture resembles breadcrumbs. Stir in the sugar and mix to a firm dough with water.
2. Roll out on a lightly floured surface and use to line a 25 cm (10 inch) china flan dish. Chill until firm, then bake 'blind' for 25-30 minutes, until golden and completely baked. Remove the baking beans and leave the pastry case until cold.
3. Dissolve the gelatine in water in a saucepan over a very gentle heat.
4. Whisk the eggs yolks and sugar until pale. Whisk in the salt and nutmeg, then stir in the cooled gelatine, brandy and Crème de cacao. Chill until just on the point of setting, stirring occasionally.
5. Whisk the egg whites until stiff. Whisk the cream to soft peaks. Fold the cream and then the egg whites into the brandy mixture. Spoon into the pastry case. Chill until set.
6. Decorate with whipped cream and chocolate curls.

Variation:
For Banana Daiquiri Pie, dissolve the gelatine in 50 ml (2 fl oz) water. Omit the nutmeg, brandy and Crème de cacao. Instead purée 1 ripe banana (peeled), 75 ml (3 fl oz) Daiquiri (white rum) and 2 tablespoons lemon juice until smooth. Use 175 ml (6 fl oz) double or whipping cream. Decorate with whipped cream and banana slices.

PECAN PIE

Serves 8
175 g (6 oz) plain flour
pinch of salt
100 g (4 oz) unsalted butter
25 g (1 oz) sugar
1 tablespoon cold water
Filling:
50 g (2 oz) pecan nuts
3 eggs
250 ml (8 fl oz) corn syrup or golden syrup
75 g (3 oz) light brown sugar
½ teaspoon vanilla essence
¼ teaspoon salt

Preparation time: 25 minutes
Cooking time: 50 minutes
Oven: 190°C, 375°F, Gas Mark 5;
220°C, 425°F, Gas Mark 7;
180°C, 350°F, Gas Mark 4

1. Sift the flour and salt into a basin. Rub in the butter then add the sugar and mix with the water to a firm dough. Roll out on a lightly floured surface and use to line a 24 cm (9½ inch) china flan dish or tin. Bake 'blind' in a preheated oven for 10 minutes. Increase the heat.
2. Remove the baking beans from the pastry case and arrange pecan nuts in circles on the base of the flan.
3. Whisk the eggs until light and frothy. Beat in the remaining ingredients and very carefully pour over the pecan nuts. They should stay in place.
4. Bake in the preheated oven at the higher temperature for 10 minutes, then reduce the heat and cook for a further 30 minutes. Allow to cool completely before serving.

Variation:
For an extra nutty pie you can chop some more pecans about 25-40 g (1-2 oz) and add these to the egg and syrup mixture. Pour this into the pastry case and then decorate with whole pecans. If pecans prove difficult to obtain use walnuts instead.

Cinnamon galette

CINNAMON GALETTE

Serves 10-12

350 g (12 oz) butter
450 g (1 lb) caster sugar
2 eggs
300 g (11 oz) plain flour
2 tablespoons ground cinnamon
900 ml (1½ pints) double or whipping cream, whipped

To decorate:

icing sugar
1 x 425 g (15 oz) can red cherries, drained or 12 fresh cherries
angelica leaves (optional)

Preparation time 45 minutes
Cooking time: 10 minutes per batch
Oven: 190°C, 375°F, Gas Mark 5

This spectacular dessert is rather time consuming but well worth the effort.

1. Cut out 14 x 23 cm (9 inch) circles of greaseproof paper. Grease each one lightly.
2. Cream the butter and sugar until pale and fluffy. Beat in the eggs and then fold in the flour sifted with the cinnamon.
3. Divide the mixture into 14 portions. Using a palette knife, spread each portion on to a circle of greaseproof paper. Work from the centre to the outside with smooth strokes. Bake these, 2 at a time, on wetted baking sheets in a preheated oven for about 10 minutes. Leave until cold, then carefully peel off the greaseproof paper.
4. Layer the cinnamon rounds, spreading each one with whipped cream. Reserve about 150 ml (5 fl oz) and use to pipe rosettes on the top of the galette. Dust the top with icing sugar and decorate with cherries and angelica leaves, (if using).

MOCHA POTS

75 g (3 oz) plain chocolate
25 g (1 oz) butter
1 tablespoon instant coffee powder
3 eggs, separated
1 tablespoon chocolate or coffee brandy-based liqueur
8 tablespoons single cream
To decorate:
whipped cream
crystallized violet petals

Preparation time: 15 minutes, plus chilling
Cooking time: 3 minutes

1. Break the chocolate into a basin. Add the butter and coffee and place the basin in a saucepan of hot water. Heat gently until melted.
2. Beat in the egg yolks until smooth. Off the heat, stir in the brandy.
3. Whisk the egg whites until stiff and fold into the chocolate mixture. Spoon into 4 coffee cups or small glasses. Chill until set.
4. Decorate each with a rosette of cream and crystallized violets. Serve at once.

HAZELNUT CREAM ROLL

Serves 6

3 eggs
75 g (3 oz) plus 3 tablespoons caster sugar
75 g (3 oz) hazelnuts, ground
2 tablespoons wholemeal flour
1 x 300 ml (10 fl oz) carton double or whipping cream
225 g (8 oz) fresh blackberries

Preparation time: 25 minutes
Cooking time: 20 minutes
Oven: 200°C, 400°F, Gas Mark 6

1. Grease and line a 33 x 23 cm (13 x 9 inch) Swiss roll tin.

2. Whisk the eggs and 75 g (3 oz) of the sugar in a basin over hot water until thick and pale, about 10 minutes.

3. Off the heat, fold in the hazelnuts and flour with a metal spoon. Spread the mixture evenly in the prepared tin and bake in a preheated oven for about 10 minutes until firm and golden.

4. Sprinkle a large piece of greaseproof paper with 2 tablespoons caster sugar. Turn the hazelnut cake on to the paper, remove the lining paper very carefully and, starting at a short end, roll up the cake with the greaseproof paper inside it. Allow to cool on a wire tray until completely cold.

5. Whip the cream. Place about a quarter in a piping bag fitted with a star nozzle.

6. Unroll the cake carefully and spread with the remaining cream. Arrange three-quarters of the blackberries on top and roll up again. Sprinkle with the remaining sugar. Trim the ends and transfer to a serving plate.

7. Decorate with whirls of cream and the remaining blackberries.

Turn the hazelnut cake on to a sheet of greaseproof paper sprinkled with caster sugar. Carefully peel away the lining paper.

While the cake is still warm, grasp the sugared paper and starting from a short edge roll the paper and the cake together. Allow to cool before filling.

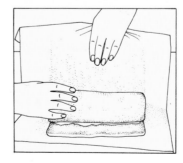

When cold unroll the cake and spread with the filling. Turn over the bottom short edge of cake. Gently lift the paper with one hand whilst carefully rolling the cake with the other.

Hazelnut cream roll; Mocha pots

STEM GINGER BAVAROIS

Serves 6
3 egg yolks
50 g (2 oz) caster sugar
400 ml (⅔ pint) milk
2 tablespoons gelatine
2 tablespoons orange juice
2 tablespoon water
4 tablespoons ginger wine
1 x 300 ml (10 fl oz) carton double or whipping cream
75 g (3 oz) stem ginger, chopped
To decorate:
whipped cream
grated orange rind

Preparation time: 20 minutes, plus chilling
Cooking time: 5 minutes

1. Whisk the egg yolks and sugar together until thick and pale.
2. Warm the milk and whisk into the egg mixture. Cook in a basin over hot water until thickened and the mixture coats the back of a wooden spoon.
3. Dissolve the gelatine in the orange juice and water over gentle heat. Stir into the egg mixture, then chill until on the point of setting.
4. Whisk the ginger wine and cream together until the cream stands in soft peaks. Fold into the egg custard, then fold in the chopped stem ginger.
5. Turn the mixture into a 1.5 litre (2½ pint) wetted charlotte tin and chill for about 4 hours until set.
6. Unmould on to a serving plate, pipe with whipped cream and decorate with grated orange rind.

ROULADE CHOCOLAT

Serves 6-8

175 g (6 oz) plain chocolate
3 tablespoons hot water
5 eggs, separated
175 g (6 oz) caster sugar
icing sugar, for dredging
450 ml (½ pint) double or whipping cream, whipped
chocolate lacework, to decorate

Preparation time: 25 minutes
Cooking time: 20-25 minutes
Oven: 180°C, 350°F, Gas Mark 4

The texture of this dessert is like a mousse rather than sponge and it cracks on rolling.

1. Grease and line a 38 x 23 cm (15 x 9 inch) Swiss roll tin.
2. Gently warm the chocolate and water together until melted and smooth.
3. Whisk the egg yolks and sugar together until thick and pale, about 10 minutes, then stir in the chocolate mixture until evenly blended.
4. Whisk the egg whites until stiff and fold into the chocolate mixture. Spoon into the prepared tin and bake in a preheated oven for 15-20 minutes until firm.
5. Cover with a sheet of greaseproof paper and a damp tea towel and leave until completely cold.
6. Turn out on to a large piece of greaseproof paper dusted with icing sugar. Remove the lining paper, spread with half the cream and roll up like a Swiss roll.
7. Place on a serving plate and pipe the remaining cream. Decorate with chocolate lacework.

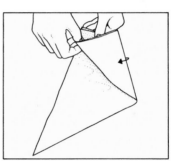
Fold a 10″ square of greaseproof paper in half. Hold the apex of the triangle and bring one corner to meet it.

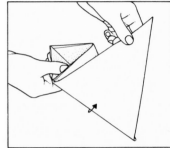
Draw the other corner around the cone, pulling it taught until a sharp point is formed.

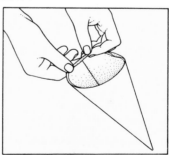
Secure the piping bag by tucking the corners inside and then making a neat double fold.

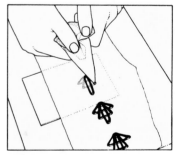
Fill the piping bag with melted chocolate. Snip off the point. Draw the lacework design on a template. Cover with non-stick silicone paper. Pipe following the stencil.

Stem ginger bavarois; Roulade chocolat

GÂTEAU PITHIVIERS

Serves 6-8

100 g (4 oz) caster sugar
100 g (4 oz) ground almonds
50 g (2 oz) butter, softened
2 egg yolks
2 tablespoons dark rum
35 g (12 oz) frozen puff pastry, thawed
15 g (½ oz) icing sugar

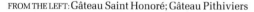

Preparation time: 15 minutes
Cooking time: 30 minutes
Oven: 200°C, 400°F, Gas Mark 6;
       240°C, 475°F, Gas Mark 9

1. Beat together the sugar, almonds, butter, egg yolks and rum.
2. Divide the pastry in 2 and roll each piece into a 23 cm (9 inch) circle. Place 1 circle on a wetted baking sheet and spread the filling in the centre to within 2 cm (¾ inch) of the edge.
3. Mark 8 crescent shape slashes in the second round, radiating from the centre to within 2.5 cm (1 inch) of the edge.
4. Moisten the edges of the first round of pastry with water. Place the second round on top. Seal the edges well, knock up and flute (page 34).
5. Bake in a preheated oven for 20 minutes. Increase the heat, dredge the top of the gâteau with icing sugar and return to the oven for 5-10 minutes until the sugar is melted, and forms a glaze on the pastry.

Make 4 crescent shaped slashes at equal intervals in the pastry. Cut between these to make a total of 8 slashes.

FROM THE LEFT: Gâteau Saint Honoré; Gâteau Pithiviers

GÂTEAU SAINT HONORÉ

Serves 8
75 g (3 oz) plain flour, sifted
50 g (2 oz) butter
25 g (1 oz) caster sugar
Choux pastry:
50 g (2 oz) butter or margarine
150 ml (¼ pint) water
65 g (2½ oz) plain flour, sifted
2 eggs, beaten
Pastry cream:
1 egg
1 egg yolk
50 g (2 oz) caster sugar
few drops of vanilla essence
2 tablespoons cornflour
2 tablespoons plain flour
300 ml (½ pint) milk
Caramel:
200 g (8 oz) sugar
100 ml (4 fl oz) water
Decoration and filling:
1 x 300 ml (½ pint) carton double or whipping cream
2 tablespoons medium sherry
1 tablespoon icing sugar
1 tablespoon pistachio nuts, skinned and chopped

Preparation time: 1 hour
Cooking time: about 1 hour
Oven: choux pastry 220°C, 425°F, Gas Mark 7
pastry base 180°C, 350°F, Gas Mark 4

1. To make the pastry base, place the flour in a mixing bowl, work in the butter and then the sugar to give a firm dough. Roll out to a 23 cm (9 inch) round and prick well with a fork. Bake in a preheated oven for about 20 minutes until golden. Leave until cold.

2. To make the choux pastry, place the butter and water in a saucepan. Heat until the butter has melted, then bring to the boil. Off the heat, immediately add all the flour and beat until the mixture forms a ball, leaving the sides of the pan clean. Allow to cool slightly, then beat in the eggs a little at a time until the mixture is smooth.

3. Spoon the paste into a piping bag fitted with a plain wide nozzle. Pipe 12 small balls and a 20 cm (8 inch) ring of pastry on a greased baking sheet. Bake in a preheated oven for 20 minutes, make slits in the bottom of the balls and the sides of the ring to allow steam to escape. Return to the oven for 10 minutes. Cool on a wire tray.

4. To make the pastry cream, beat the egg, egg yolk, sugar, vanilla essence, cornflour and flour together. Heat the milk and pour on to the egg mixture, stirring. Return to the pan and cook, stirring until thickened. Leave until cold. Spoon into a piping bag fitted with a plain nozzle.

5. Place the pastry base on a plate. Cut the choux ring in half and fill the choux and ring with pastry cream.

6. Dissolve the sugar in the water over a gentle heat, then cook until caramel in colour. Remove from the heat. Using tongs, quickly dip each choux ball in caramel and place on the ring. Spoon any extra caramel over the balls.

7. Place the ring on top of the pastry base. Whip the cream with the sherry and icing sugar and spoon into the centre of the ring. Sprinkle with the nuts and chill.

Adding the flour all at once.

Beating to form a ball.

Beating in eggs.

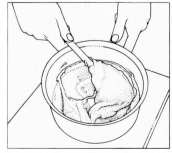
Beating pastry until smooth.

NECTARINE VACHERIN

Serves 12-14

50 g (2 oz) hazelnuts, toasted
6 egg whites
350 g (12 oz) caster sugar
450 ml (15 fl oz) whipping cream, whipped
6 nectarines, stoned and sliced

Preparation time: 30 minutes
Cooking time: 1-1¼ hours
Oven: 140°C, 275°F, Gas Mark 1

1. Grind or grate the hazelnuts in a rotary grater.
2. Draw a 23 cm (9 inch) circle on each of 3 pieces of non-stick silicone paper or greaseproof paper. Place the paper on baking sheets. Lightly oil the greaseproof paper.
3. Whisk the egg whites until stiff, then whisk in the sugar, a tablespoon at a time, until stiff and glossy. Fold in the prepared hazelnuts with a metal spoon.
4. Spread the hazelnut meringue (or pipe with a large plain nozzle) over the 3 circles.
5. Bake in a preheated oven for 1-1¼ hours until crisp and dry. Leave to cool, then peel off the paper.
6. Layer the meringue rounds with whipped cream and nectarines, finishing with cream and nectarines to decorate the top.

There has always been a lot of discussion about how to make meringues – they are in fact very simple if you follow a few basic rules.

Make sure all equipment is really clean and free from grease. Use a little lemon juice or vinegar to clean the mixing bowl and whisk. A pinch of salt added to *fresh* egg whites helps to stabilise them. Whisk the egg whites until they are really stiff – you should be able to turn the bowl upside down without the egg whites dropping out. Whisk in the sugar about 1 tablespoon at a time whisking well between each addition until the meringue is thick, white and glossy. A squeeze of lemon juice added to the meringue will give extra stability. Fold in any flavourings such as chopped nuts or strong liquid coffee with a metal spoon.

Dried out meringues will store well for several months in a cool dry place. Wrap in foil or simply store in a rigid plastic container.

Variation: use alternative fruits – raspberries are particularly good.

HAZELNUT MERINGUES WITH COFFEE CREAM

Serves 8-10
4 egg whites
225 g (8 oz) caster sugar
50 g (2 oz) hazelnuts, finely ground or grated
1 x 300 ml (10 fl oz) carton double or whipping cream
2 teaspoons instant coffee, dissolved in 1 teaspoon boiling water
chocolate curls, to decorate (optional)

Preparation time: 30 minutes, plus cooling
Cooking time: 2 hours
Oven: 120°C, 250°F, Gas Mark ½

1. Whisk the egg whites until stiff, then whisk in the sugar a tablespoon at a time until all is used up and the mixture is thick and glossy. Fold in the hazelnuts with a metal spoon.
2. Spoon 16 oval shapes of meringue on to baking sheets lined with non-stick silicone paper or lightly oiled greaseproof paper. Bake in a preheated oven for about 2 hours until well dried out (they will lift easily from the paper). Leave until cold on a wire tray.
3. Whip the cream until stiff, fold in the coffee and use to sandwich the meringues. Decorate with chocolate curls, (page 16) if using.

BAKED STUFFED PEACHES

50 g (2 oz) sponge cake, crumbled
75 g (3 oz) ground almonds
grated rind and juice of 1 medium orange
4 large ripe peaches or nectarines
2 tablespoons caster sugar
25 g (1 oz) butter
150 ml (¼ pint) sweet white wine

Preparation time: 15 minutes
Cooking time: 15-20 minutes
Oven: 180°C, 350°F, Gas Mark 4

1. Mix the sponge cake, ground almonds, orange rind and juice together to a paste.
2. Halve and stone the peaches and pipe or spoon some almond mixture on top of each peach half.
3. Place in a buttered ovenproof dish in a single layer, sprinkle with sugar and dot with butter.
4. Pour the white wine into the dish and bake in a preheated oven for 15-20 minutes. Serve at once.

KIWI FRUIT PAVLOVA

Serves 8
4 egg whites
225 g (8 oz) caster sugar
1 teaspoon vanilla essence
1 teaspoon vinegar
2 teaspoons cornflour
450 ml (15 fl oz) whipping cream, whipped
6 kiwi fruits, peeled and sliced

Preparation time: 20 minutes
Cooking time: 1 hour
Oven: 150°C, 300°F, Gas Mark 2

This is the classic dessert to emerge from Australia. It is very similar to a meringue, except that cornflour, vinegar and vanilla essence are added to the egg white. This together with the shorter cooking time produces a crisp exterior and a 'marshmallowy' centre.

Many other fresh fruits may be used instead of kiwis – try a combination of strawberry, pineapple and passion fruit or mango and canned or fresh lychees, decorated with tiny mint leaves.

1. Mark a 23 cm (9 inch) circle on sheet of non-stick silicone paper or greaseproof paper. Place the paper on a baking sheet. Lightly oil the greaseproof paper.
2. Whisk the egg whites in a large basin until stiff. Continue whisking, adding the sugar a tablespoon at a time until the mixture is thick and glossy and all the sugar is used up.
3. Fold in the vanilla essence, vinegar and cornflour and spoon the mixture inside the marked circle to give a neat shape. Make a slight 'well' in the centre with the outside edge slightly higher.
4. Bake in a preheated oven for 1 hour. Cool, transfer carefully to a serving plate.
5. Decorate with whipped cream and kiwi fruit slices.

Kiwi fruit pavlova; Hazelnut meringues with Coffee cream;
Baked stuffed peaches

RUM AND RAISIN GÂTEAU

Serves 8
5 eggs, separated
150 g (5 oz) caster sugar
1 teaspoon grated orange rind
1 tablespoon orange juice
1 tablespoon rum
100 g (4 oz) fine semolina
50 g (2 oz) ground almonds
pinch of salt
Filling:
50 g (2 oz) raisins
3 tablespoons rum
1 large orange
1 x 300 ml (½ pint) carton double or whipping cream
3 tablespoons icing sugar

Preparation time: 25 minutes
Cooking time: 45 minutes
Oven: 180°C, 350°F, Gas Mark 4

1. Whisk the egg yolks and sugar together until thick and pale. Whisk in the orange rind and juice and the rum. Fold in the semolina and ground almonds.
2. Whisk the egg whites with a pinch of salt until stiff. Fold into the egg yolk mixture with a metal spoon.
3. Pour the mixture into a greased and floured 20 cm (8 inch) spring form tin. Bake in a preheated oven for 45 minutes, until risen and golden and firm to the touch.
4. When cool, remove from the tin and leave on a wire tray until cold. Split the cake into 2 layers.
5. To make the filling, roughly chop the raisins and soak them in the rum for as long as possible.
6. Peel the orange, removing all the white pith. Remove the orange segments (page 24) and reserve for decoration. Reserve the juice.
7. Whip the cream until stiff, then stir in the reserved orange juice, 2 tablespoons icing sugar and the rum from the soaked raisins. Reserve one-third of the cream and spoon into a piping bag fitted with a star nozzle.
8. Fold the raisins into the remaining cream and use to sandwich the 2 layers of cake together. Dust the top of the cake with icing sugar and pipe with the reserved rum-flavoured cream. Decorate with orange segments.

CRÊPES SUZETTE

Serves 6
75 g (3 oz) plain flour
pinch of salt
2 tablespoons caster sugar
1 egg
1 egg yolk
250 ml (8 fl oz) milk
2 tablespoons melted butter
oil for frying pancakes
Orange butter:
100 g (4 oz) butter
100 g (4 oz) caster sugar
grated rind and juice of 1 orange
1 tablespoon orange liqueur
4 tablespoons brandy

Preparation time: about 45 minutes
Cooking time: about 30 minutes

1. Sift the flour and salt together. Stir in the sugar. Add the egg and egg yolk and beat in the milk, a little at a time to give a smooth batter. Stir in the melted butter.
2. Heat a little oil in an 18 cm (7 inch) frying pan and make 12 pancakes. Keep warm.
3. For the orange butter, cream the butter and sugar until pale and fluffy. Beat in the orange rind and juice and the orange liqueur.
4. Fold the pancakes into 'cornets' and spoon a little orange butter into each one.
5. Place the remaining orange butter in a large frying pan. Arrange the pancakes in the pan and heat gently until the butter has melted.
6. Warm the brandy in a small saucepan, pour over the pancakes, ignite carefully and serve at once.

To make pancakes, warm a frying pan (use either a non-stick pan or one that has been well seasoned) over medium heat. Pour in ½ teaspoon of oil and allow it to get hot (you can use butter, allow it to sizzle). Holding the frying pan on the tilt, pour in about 2 tablespoons batter, enough to just cover the base. Swirl the batter around the pan to cover the base, spreading the mixture evenly. Cook for about 1 minute until golden brown, turn over with a palette knife or fish slice or 'toss' the pancake. Cook for a further minute until golden. To keep the pancakes warm, cover with foil and place in a low oven or over a pan of simmering water.

American baked cheesecake; Rum and raisin gâteau

AMERICAN BAKED CHEESECAKE

Serves 10-12

175 g (6 oz) digestive biscuits, crushed
75 g (3 oz) butter, melted
1 kg (2 lb) full fat soft cream cheese
250 g (9 oz) caster sugar
4 eggs
40 g (1½ oz) plain flour
1 x 300 ml (10 fl oz) carton soured cream
grated rind of 1 lemon
fresh strawberries or cherries (optional)

Preparation time: 20 minutes, plus cooling
Cooking time: 45 minutes
Oven: 180°C, 350°F, Gas Mark 4

1. Mix the biscuit crumbs with the melted butter. Press into the base of a 23 cm (9 inch) spring form tin. Bake in a preheated oven for 10 minutes.
2. Beat together all the remaining ingredients except the strawberries. Pour on to the biscuit base and return to the oven for 35 minutes. Switch off the oven and leave the cheesecake in it for 2 hours.
3. Remove from the oven and leave until cold. Unmould on to a serving plate and serve with strawberries or cherries, as preferred.

HOT PUDDINGS

BREAD AND BUTTER PUDDING

40 g (1½ oz) butter
4 slices white bread, crusts removed
4 tablespoons apricot jam
25 g (1 oz) cut mixed peel
25 g (1 oz) sultanas
450 ml (¾ pint) milk
2 tablespoons sugar
2 eggs, beaten

Preparation time: 10 minutes, plus soaking
Cooking time: about 55-60 minutes
Oven: 180°C, 350°F, Gas Mark 4;
      190°C, 375°C, Gas Mark 5

1. Use 15 g (½ oz) of the butter to grease a 1.2 litre (2 pint) ovenproof serving dish.
2. Butter the bread and spread with apricot jam. Cut into small triangles. Layer the bread in the dish, sprinkling mixed peel and sultanas between the layers.
3. Heat the milk and sugar to just below boiling point. Whisk in the eggs, then strain over the bread and butter. Leave to soak for 30 minutes.
4. Place the dish in a water bath (a roasting tin with water to come at least halfway up the sides of the dish). Bake in a preheated oven for 45 minutes, then increase the heat and cook for a further 10-15 minutes until crisp and golden on top and just set. Serve at once.

BAKED PEARS IN WHITE WINE

Serves 6
50 g (2 oz) butter
6 large ripe pears (preferably Conference) peeled, halved and
    cored
6 tablespoons ginger marmalade
6 tablespoons roughly crushed macaroons
300 ml (½ pint) sweet white wine

Preparation time: 15 minutes
Cooking time: 20-30 minutes
Oven: 180°C, 350°F, Gas Mark 4

SPICED BREAD PUDDING

Serves 6-8
225 g (8 oz) stale granary bread, cubed
450 ml (¾ pint) milk
50 g (2 oz) butter
50 g (2 oz) demerara sugar
50 g (2 oz) sultanas
50 g (2 oz) currants
1 teaspoon ground cinnamon
1 teaspoon ground ginger
½ teaspoon ground nutmeg
2 eggs, beaten
demerara sugar, for sprinkling

Preparation time: 5 minutes, plus soaking
Cooking time: 45 minutes
Oven: 180°C, 350°F, Gas Mark 4

1. Place the bread in a mixing bowl. Bring the milk, butter and sugar to the boil and pour over the bread. Mix well and leave to soak for 15 minutes, stirring the mixture occasionally.
2. Add the remaining ingredients and beat well until evenly mixed.
3. Spoon into a buttered 28 x 18 cm (11 x 7 inch) ovenproof baking dish and bake in a preheated oven for 45 minutes until golden and firm to the touch. Sprinkle with demerara sugar and serve cut in squares.

1. Use a quarter of the butter to grease a large, shallow ovenproof dish, just large enough to hold the pears in a single layer.
2. Place the pear halves in the dish, cut side up, and fill the hollows with ginger marmalade and the crushed macaroons.
3. Pour the wine around the pears, dot them with the remaining butter and bake in a preheated oven for 20-30 minutes until just tender when tested with a skewer.

CLOCKWISE FROM THE LEFT: Spiced bread pudding;
Bread and butter pudding; Baked pears in white wine

ANNIE'S APPLE PIE

Serves 6

500 g (1¼ lb) cooking apples, peeled, cored and sliced
75 g (3 oz) plus 1 tablespoon caster sugar
225 g (8 oz) self-raising flour, sifted
175 g (6 oz) butter
1 egg, separated
1 tablespoon milk
2 tablespoons apricot jam
50 g (2 oz) ground almonds

Preparation time: 30 minutes
Cooking time: 40 minutes
Oven: 200°C, 400°F, Gas Mark 6

1. Place the apples and the sugar in a saucepan and simmer gently until pulpy. Cool.
2. Place the flour in a basin, rub in the butter, then mix to a firm dough with the egg yolk and milk. Chill.
3. Roll out a generous half of the pastry and use to line a 20 cm (8 inch) loose bottomed sandwich tin or flan tin. Spread the base with apricot jam.
4. Sprinkle half the ground almonds over the jam. Spread the apple filling on top and then the remaining ground almonds.
5. Top with the reserved pastry, seal the edges well and cut a couple of slits in the top of the pastry.
6. Brush the pastry with beaten egg white and sprinkle with a little sugar. Bake in a preheated oven for about 30 minutes until golden brown. Serve the pie warm with single cream.

FRIAR'S OMELETTE

Serves 6

450 g (1 lb) cooking apples, peeled, cored and sliced
grated rind and juice of ½ lemon
75 g (3 oz) sugar
1 egg, beaten
150 g (5 oz) butter
225 g (8 oz) fresh white breadcrumbs
50 g (2 oz) demerara sugar

Preparation time: 20 minutes
Cooking time: 40 minutes
Oven: 200°C, 400°F, Gas Mark 6

WHOLE BAKED BANANAS IN PUFF PASTRY WITH WALNUT RUM SAUCE

1 x 212 g (7½ oz) packet frozen puff pastry, thawed
4 medium, firm, ripe bananas, peeled
1 egg white, beaten
1 tablespoon sugar
Sauce:
200 ml (⅓ pint) water
75 g (3 oz) light brown sugar
50 g (2 oz) butter
25 g (1 oz) shelled walnuts, chopped
2 tablespoons dark rum

Preparation time: 20 minutes
Cooking time: 15-20 minutes
Oven: 220°C, 425°F, Gas Mark 7

1. Divide the pastry into 4 pieces. Roll out each piece very thinly and large enough to encase a banana.
2. Wrap the bananas in pastry, sealing the edges well with water and cutting away any excess pastry. Reserve the trimmings.
3. Re-roll the trimmings to make four thin 'ribbons' about 25 cm (10 inches) long. Wrap a pastry ribbon around each banana and form into a bow.
4. Place the bananas on a wetted baking sheet. Brush with egg white and sprinkle with sugar. Bake in a preheated oven for 15-20 minutes until crisp and golden.
5. For the sauce, place the water and sugar in a saucepan and heat gently until the sugar dissolves. Boil rapidly for about 5 minutes until slightly syrupy. Off the heat, stir in the remaining ingredients. Stir until the butter is melted. Serve immediately with the bananas.

1. Place the apples, lemon rind and juice and sugar in a saucepan. Simmer gently until 'pulpy'. Remove from the heat and beat in the egg and 25 g (1 oz) of the butter. Cool.
2. Melt the remaining butter and mix with the breadcrumbs and demerara sugar.
3. Press half the crumb mixture on to the base of a 23 cm (9 inch) ovenproof dish. Spread the apple mixture on top, then finish with the remaining crumb mixture. Press down gently.
4. Bake in a preheated oven for 30 minutes. Cool for 5 minutes, then turn out on to a serving plate. Serve with vanilla ice cream.

Whole baked bananas in puff pastry with Walnut rum sauce;
Plum dumplings

PLUM DUMPLINGS

8 firm red plums
8 teaspoons caster sugar
225 g (8 oz) shortcrust pastry
milk
caster sugar, to glaze

Preparation time: 15 minutes
Cooking time: 20-25 minutes
Oven: 200°C, 400°F, Gas Mark 6

1. Carefully split each plum and remove the stone. Fill one half with a teaspoon of caster sugar and replace the other half.
2. Divide the pastry into 8 pieces. On a lightly floured surface roll out each piece and use to form a square, large enough to enclose a plum. Trim the edges. Draw the corners of the pastry to the centre and seal the edges well with water. Decorate each dumpling with pastry leaves made from the trimmings.
3. Place the dumplings standing upright on a greased baking sheet. Brush with milk and sprinkle with caster sugar. Bake in a preheated oven for 20-25 minutes until crisp and golden on the outside and just tender in the centre when checked with a skewer.
4. Serve at once with single cream.

ALMOND AND PEAR CRÊPES

100 g (4 oz) plain flour
2 teaspoons icing sugar
1 egg
150 ml (¼ pint) milk
150 ml (¼ pint) water
2 tablespoons melted butter
oil for frying
Filling:
100 g (4 oz) butter, softened
50 g (2 oz) icing sugar, sifted
50 g (2 oz) ground almonds
1 x 425 g (15 oz) can pear halves

Preparation time: 25 minutes
Cooking time: about 20 minutes

These sweet batter pancakes are first fried then finished with a fruity, almond-rich filling.

1. Sift the flour and icing sugar into a basin. Add the egg and milk and beat to a smooth, thick batter. Stir in the water and melted butter.
2. Make 8 pancakes, (page 54) with the batter. Keep warm.
3. Beat together the butter and icing sugar until fluffy. Beat in the ground almonds.
4. Drain the pears, reserving the syrup. Chop the pears roughly and stir into the almond butter.
5. Fold the pancakes in half and spoon a little filling on to each. Roll into cornet shapes and arrange in a buttered dish.
6. Spoon over a little of the reserved syrup and place under a preheated medium grill until the pancakes turn golden brown. Serve at once.

RASPBERRY CLAFOUTIS

Serves 4-6

40 g (1½ oz) butter
3 eggs
50 g (2 oz) caster sugar
pinch of salt
65 g (2½ oz) plain flour, sifted
300 ml (½ pint) milk
225 g (8 oz) frozen raspberries
caster sugar, to sprinkle

Preparation time: 15 minutes
Cooking time: about 45 minutes
Oven: 200°C, 400°F, Gas Mark 6

Clafoutis is a thick fruit pancake, baked in the oven and served warm. It originates from the Limousin area in France, and is traditionally made with black cherries.

1. Melt the butter and use a little to grease a 23 cm (9 inch) china flan dish.
2. Whisk the eggs and sugar for about 5 minutes until pale and foamy. Stir in the salt, flour and then the milk, and the remaining melted butter to give a smooth batter.
3. Pour half the batter into the flan dish and bake in a preheated oven for 15 minutes.
4. Arrange the frozen raspberries on top of the batter and pour the remaining batter carefully around the fruit. Return to the oven for about 30 minutes until slightly risen and golden.
5. Sprinkle with caster sugar and serve at once, with thick cream.

SAUCER PANCAKES

Serves 6

50 g (2 oz) butter
50 g (2 oz) caster sugar
2 eggs
50 g (2 oz) strong plain flour, sifted
450 ml (¾ pint) milk
6 tablespoons strawberry or raspberry jam
1 x 150 ml (5 fl oz) carton double or whipping cream, whipped

Preparation time: 7-8 minutes
Cooking time: 15-20 minutes
Oven: 190°C, 375°F, Gas Mark 5

This unusual method of making pancakes is simple to do and cuts out any unpleasant frying smells. The pancake mixture is enriched with butter and sweetened with sugar. Serve with a home-made jam of your choice, such as strawberry, raspberry or blackcurrant.

1. Cream the butter and sugar until light and fluffy. Beat in the eggs and then the flour.
2. Butter 6 large saucers and place on baking sheets. Divide the batter between them.
3. Bake in a preheated oven for 15-20 minutes until set and golden. Serve immediately with a spoonful of jam and a spoonful of cream on top.

FROM THE LEFT: Almond and pear crêpes; Raspberry clafoutis

APRICOT AND ALMOND SPONGE PUDDING

Serves 6

75 g (3 oz) butter or margarine, softened
100 g (4 oz) caster sugar
2 eggs, beaten
few drops of almond essence
100 g (4 oz) self-raising flour, sifted
50 g (2 oz) ground almonds
a little milk (if necessary)
1 x 425 g (15 oz) can apricot halves, drained
6 whole blanched almonds

Preparation time: 15 minutes
Cooking time: 1¾-2 hours

1. Grease a 900 ml (2 pint) pudding basin.
2. Cream the butter and sugar until light and fluffy, then beat in the eggs and almond essence.
3. Fold in the flour and ground almonds, and moisten with milk, if necessary, to give a dropping consistency.
4. Place 6 apricot halves, cut side up, with an almond in the centre of each, on the base of the pudding basin.
5. Roughly chop the remaining apricots and fold into the sponge mixture. Spoon into the basin and cover with buttered foil with a centre pleat.
6. Steam for 1¾-2 hours until firm to the touch. Turn out on to a serving plate and serve with custard or cream.

STICKY PRUNE PUDDING

Serves 4-6
100 g (4 oz) prunes
100 g (4 oz) dark brown sugar
100 ml (3½ fl oz) oil
2 eggs
150 g (5 oz) brown flour
½ teaspoon bicarbonate of soda
½ teaspoon cinnamon
½ teaspoon mixed spice
100 ml (3½ fl oz) buttermilk
25 g (1 oz) shredded coconut
Topping:
50 g (2 oz) dark brown sugar
2 tablespoons golden syrup
4 tablespoons buttermilk

Preparation time: 25 minutes
Cooking time: 1 hour
Oven: 180°C, 350°F, Gas Mark 4

1. Place the prunes in a small saucepan. Just cover with water and simmer for 10 minutes. Drain and remove the stones. Roughly chop the prunes.
2. Whisk the sugar, oil and eggs together for 10 minutes until pale and thick.
3. Beat in the remaining ingredients and the prunes and transfer the mixture to a greased 1.2 litre (2 pint) buttered shallow ovenproof dish.
4. Bake in a preheated oven for about 50 minutes until risen and firm to the touch.
5. For the topping, place the sugar and golden syrup in a saucepan over gentle heat until the sugar dissolves. Off the heat, stir in the buttermilk.
6. Prick the surface of the pudding with a skewer and pour over the topping. Leave for 5 minutes to soak in, then serve at once with fresh cream or ice cream.

ALMOND AND FIG SPONGE PUDDING

Serves 6
100 g (4 oz) butter
75 g (3 oz) caster sugar
2 eggs, beaten
grated rind of ½ lemon
100 g (4 oz) self-raising flour, sifted
100 g (4 oz) marzipan, diced
a little milk, (if necessary)
1 x 425 g (15 oz) can figs, drained

Preparation time: 15 minutes
Cooking time: 1¾-2 hours

LEFT: Apricot and almond sponge pudding; RIGHT: Almond and fig sponge pudding

VIENNA PUDDING

Serves 6
butter, for greasing
90 g (3½ oz) sugar
2 tablespoons water
300 ml (½ pint) milk
100 g (4 oz) stale bread, crusts removed and diced
2 tablespoons medium sherry
100 g (4 oz) sultanas
50 g (2 oz) cut mixed peel
25 g (1 oz) almonds, chopped
2 eggs
grated rind of ½ lemon

Preparation time: 15 minutes, plus soaking
Cooking time: 1 hour

1. Butter a 1.2 litre (2 pint) pudding basin and sprinkle with 15 g (½ oz) of the sugar to coat the inside.
2. Dissolve 25 g (1 oz) of the remaining sugar in the water over medium heat and cook until caramel coloured. Add the milk immediately and stir until the caramel is dissolved.
3. Place the bread in a basin and sprinkle with sherry. Add the sultanas, mixed peel and almonds.
4. Beat together the remaining sugar, eggs and lemon rind, beat in the caramel milk and then stir in the bread and fruit. Pour into the pudding basin and leave to soak for 30 minutes.
5. Cover the basin with buttered foil with a centre pleat and steam over boiling water for 1 hour until firm to the touch.
6. Turn out and serve with cream.

1. Grease a 900 ml (2 pint) pudding basin.
2. Cream the butter and sugar until light and fluffy, then beat in the eggs and lemon rind.
3. Fold in the flour and moisten with milk, if necessary, to give a dropping consistency. Stir in the diced marzipan.
4. Arrange sufficient fig halves to cover the base of the pudding basin. Spoon in half the sponge mixture and level the surface.
5. Make a second layer of figs and finish with the remaining sponge mixture.
6. Cover with buttered foil with a centre pleat. Steam for 1¾-2 hours until firm to the touch. Turn out on to a serving plate and serve with custard or cream.

SUSSEX POND PUDDING

Serves 4-6

225 g (8 oz) self-raising flour, sifted
100 g (4 oz) shredded suet
about 8 tablespoons cold water
100 g (4 oz) butter, softened
100 g (4 oz) light brown sugar
100 g (4 oz) currants
1 small thin-skinned lemon, washed and dried

Preparation time: 15 minutes
Cooking time: 2 hours

1. Place the flour and suet in a basin. Add sufficient cold water to mix to a firm dough.
2. On a lightly floured surface roll out the pastry and use to line a 1.5 litre (2½ pint) buttered pudding basin. Reserve the cut section.
3. Cream the butter and sugar until light and fluffy. Stir in the currants. Prick the lemon all over the surface with a skewer.
4. Spoon a little of the currant mixture into the pudding basin. Press the lemon in the centre and pack the remaining currant mixture around it.
5. Roll out the remaining pastry to make a lid. Dampen the edges with water and place on top of the pudding. Seal the edges well.
6. Cover with buttered foil with a centre pleat and steam in a saucepan of boiling water for 2 hours.
7. Unmould and serve at once with custard.

Roll the pastry into a circle about 4″ larger than the top of the basin. Cut out a quarter and reserve.

Ease the pastry into the basin. Dampen the edges and seal firmly.

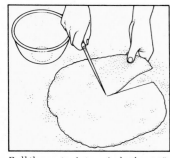

Roll out the reserved pastry to form a lid. Fold the pastry edges over the filling.

Dampen the edges of the pastry and the lid and seal firmly.

RICH CHRISTMAS PUDDING

Serves 10-12

175 g (6 oz) plain flour
1 teaspoon mixed spice
1 teaspoon ground nutmeg
1 teaspoon ground cinnamon
50 g (2 oz) fresh white breadcrumbs
100 g (4 oz) shredded suet
100 g (4 oz) brown sugar
100 g (4 oz) sultanas
100 g (4 oz) currants
100 g (4 oz) raisins
100 g (4 oz) cut mixed peel
100 g (4 oz) almonds, chopped
100 g (4 oz) carrot, grated
100 g (4 oz) apple, grated
2 eggs, beaten
grated rind and juice of 1 small orange
150 ml (¼ pint) Guiness
3 tablespoons brandy or rum, to flame (optional)

Preparation time: 20 minutes
Cooking time: 4 hours, then 1 hour before serving

1. Sift the flour and spices into a large mixing bowl. Add the dry ingredients, carrot and apple. Stir well.
2. Stir in the eggs, grated orange rind and juice and Guinness. Mix together well. Cover and leave overnight in a cool place.
3. Spoon into a lightly greased 1.8 litre (3 pint) pudding basin. Cover with buttered foil with a centre pleat and steam in a saucepan of boiling water for 4 hours. Check the water level from time to time. Leave until cold, wrap in greaseproof paper and then foil and store in a cool, dry place for up to 3 months.
4. To serve, re-steam for 1 hour. Turn out the pudding and serve at once.
5. Alternatively, use two 900 ml (1½ pint) pudding basins. Steam for 2 hours and re-heat for 30-45 minutes.
6. To flame the pudding, warm the brandy or rum in a small saucepan. Pour the alcohol over the pudding and ignite immediately.

Rich Christmas pudding

PINEAPPLE CANARY PUDDING

Serves 4-6

1 x 250 g (9 oz) can pineapple
100 g (4 oz) butter
100 g (4 oz) light brown sugar
2 eggs, beaten
175 g (6 oz) self-raising flour, sifted
grated rind of 1 lemon

Preparation time: 15 minutes
Cooking time: 1½ hours

1. Drain the pineapple, reserving the syrup. Roughly chop the fruit.
2. Cream the butter and sugar until light and fluffy. Beat in the eggs, then fold in the flour and then the pineapple and lemon rind.
3. Add a little of the pineapple syrup, if necessary, to give a 'dropping' consistency.
4. Spoon the mixture into a greased 900 ml (1½ pint) pudding basin. Cover with a piece of buttered foil with a centre pleat and steam over boiling water for about 1½ hours until risen and firm to the touch.
5. Turn out and serve with custard.

Variation:
For Banana and Chocolate Chip Pudding, omit the pineapple and lemon rind. Add 1 banana, peeled and chopped, 50 g (2 oz) chopped chocolate and 25 g (1 oz) chopped walnuts at step 2. Moisten with milk and steam.

SURPRISE LEMON PUDDING

Serves 6

3 eggs, separated
grated rind and juice of 1 large lemon
250 ml (8 fl oz) milk
175 g (6 oz) caster sugar
pinch of salt
25 g (1 oz) plain flour, sifted

Preparation time: 10 minutes
Cooking time: 30 minutes
Oven: 160°C, 325°F, Gas Mark 3

1. Combine all the ingredients except the egg whites until evenly mixed.
2. Whisk the egg whites until stiff, then fold in the lemon mixture.
3. Turn the mixture into a greased 1.5 litre (2½ pint) ovenproof dish and bake in a preheated oven for about 30 minutes until the top is risen and golden. Serve at once.

DUKE OF CAMBRIDGE TART

Serves 6

175 g (6 oz) shortcrust pastry
75 g (3 oz) butter
50 g (2 oz) caster sugar
1 egg (size 2), beaten
100 g (4 oz) mixed crystallized fruit, chopped

Preparation time: 10 minutes
Cooking time: 20-25 minutes
Oven: 180°C, 350°F, Gas Mark 4

1. Roll out the pastry on a lightly floured surface, and use to line a 20 cm (8 inch) flan tin.
2. Place the butter, sugar and egg in a small saucepan. Bring to the boil, stirring all the time. Immediately take off the heat, stir in the crystallized fruit and pour into the pastry case.
3. Bake in a preheated oven for 20-25 minutes until set and golden. Serve warm.

NEW YORK NOODLE PUDDING

Serves 6
100 g (4 oz) ribbon noodles
50 g (2 oz) butter, melted
2 eggs, separated
75 g (3 oz) plus 2 tablespoons caster sugar
100 g (4 oz) soured cream
100 g (4 oz) skimmed milk soft cheese
1 teaspoon vanilla essence
200 ml (⅓ pint) milk
½ teaspoon ground cinnamon

Preparation time: 20 minutes
Cooking time: 40-45 minutes
Oven: 190°C, 375°F, Gas Mark 5

This is a warm and filling pudding.

1. Cook the noodles in boiling water for 10 minutes. Drain, rinse and drain well. Mix with the butter and transfer to a 1.5 litre (2½ pint) shallow ovenproof dish.
2. Beat the egg yolks with 75 g (3 oz) sugar, the soured cream, soft cheese and vanilla until smooth. Slowly stir in the milk.
3. Whisk the egg whites until stiff and fold into the yolk mixture. Pour over the noodles.
4. Mix the caster sugar and cinnamon together and sprinkle over the top of the pudding. Bake in a preheated oven for about 40-45 minutes until firm and just set. Serve warm.

FRENCH PLUM PUDDING

Serves 6-8
175 g (6 oz) plain flour
175 g (6 oz) butter
75 g (3 oz) caster sugar
50 g (2 oz) ground almonds
1 egg yolk
1 tablespoon cold water
750 g (1½ lb) plums, halved and stoned

Preparation time: 15 minutes
Cooking time: 30-35 minutes
Oven: 200°C, 400°F, Gas Mark 6

PRUNE AND ALMOND BAKED CREAM

225 g (8 oz) pitted prunes, soaked overnight
about 25 whole almonds
3 eggs, separated
75 g (3 oz) sugar
1 x 150 ml (5 fl oz) carton single cream
1 x 150 ml (5 fl oz) carton double cream
50 g (2 oz) butter
1 tablespoon port
few drops of almond essence

Preparation time: 25 minutes, plus cooling
Cooking time: about 1¼ hours
Oven: 180°C, 350°F, Gas Mark 4

1. Simmer the prunes in the minimum of water for about 10 minutes until tender and 'plumped'. Allow to cool in the liquid, then drain and place an almond in the centre of each prune.
2. Arrange the prunes in a single layer, in a buttered 1.5 litre (2½ pint) ovenproof serving dish.
3. Beat the egg yolks and sugar until thick and pale. Warm the creams and butter together until the butter is just melted. Whisk into the egg mixture. Stir in the port and almond essence. Whisk the egg whites until stiff and fold into the mixture.
4. Pour the egg mixture over the prunes and place in a water bath (a roasting tin with water to come halfway up the sides of the dish). Bake in a preheated oven for about 1 hour until slightly risen and golden.

1. Sift the flour into a mixing bowl. Rub in two-thirds of the butter, then stir in 25 g (1 oz) of the sugar and the ground almonds. Mix to a firm dough with the egg yolk and water. Chill until required.
2. Melt the remaining butter in a 23 cm (9 inch) round flameproof dish. Add the remaining sugar and stir until caramelized.
3. Off the heat, arrange the plums, skin side down, over the base of the dish.
4. Roll out the pastry, on a lightly floured surface, into a round just over 23 cm (9 inches). Place on top of the plums, pressing down gently and tucking in at the edges. Bake in a preheated oven for 30-35 minutes until golden. Leave for 5 minutes, then turn out on to a serving dish. Serve at once.

CLOCKWISE FROM THE LEFT: New York noodle pudding;
Duke of Cambridge tart; French plum pudding

SYRUPY UPSIDE DOWN PUDDING

Serves 6

1 x 425 g (15 oz) can pineapples rings in natural juice
50 g (2 oz) butter
50 g (2 oz) light brown sugar
6 glacé or maraschino cherries
2 eggs
50 g (2 oz) caster sugar
50 g (2 oz) plain flour, sifted

Preparation time: 20 minutes
Cooking time: 35 minutes
Oven: 200°C, 400°F, Gas Mark 6

1. Drain the pineapple and place the juice in a saucepan with the butter and light brown sugar. Boil rapidly for 10 minutes until fairly syrupy.
2. Arrange the pineapple rings in a greased 24 cm (9½ inch) ovenproof dish or sandwich tin. Place a cherry in the centre of each pineapple ring.
3. Whisk the eggs and sugar for about 10 minutes until pale and thick. Fold in the flour.
4. Spoon the cooled syrup over the pineapple and pour the sponge mixture carefully on top.
5. Bake in a preheated oven for 25 minutes until risen and firm to the touch.
6. Unmould on to a serving plate and serve at once.

Variation:
For Apricot Upside Down Pudding, use 1 x 425 g (15 oz) can apricot halves in natural juice instead of pineapple. Boil the syrup for about 5 minutes. Cut each cherry into 3 slices and place a piece in the centre of each apricot half. Place cut side down in the dish. Continue as above.

TOFFEE APPLE PUDDING

Serves 4-6

225 g (8 oz) self-raising flour
pinch of salt
100 g (4 oz) shredded suet
about 6 tablespoons water
50 g (2 oz) butter, softened
100 g (4 oz) soft brown sugar
750 g (1½ lb) cooking apples, peeled, cored and thinly sliced

Preparation time: 15 minutes
Cooking time: 50 minutes-1 hour
Oven: 180°C, 350°F, Gas Mark 4

FROM THE LEFT: Toffee apple pudding; Syrupy upside down pudding

1. Sift the flour and salt into a basin. Stir in the suet and mix to a firm dough with water.
2. Mix the butter and half the sugar and spread over the base and sides of a 900 ml (1½ pint) pie dish.
3. On a lightly floured surface roll out half the pastry and use to line the pie dish. Do not trim the edges. Fill with half the apples and sprinkle with the remaining sugar. Add the remaining apples and press down gently.
4. Fold the pastry edges in towards the centre of the dish. Roll out the remaining pastry, brush lightly with water and place damp side down on the apples. Tuck in the edges.
5. Bake in a preheated oven for about 1 hour until the pastry is golden and the apples are tender when tested with a skewer. Leave for 5 minutes, then turn out on to a plate. Serve at once.

TIPSY DATE PUDDING

100 g (4 oz) stoned dates, chopped
150 ml (¼ pint) boiling water
½ teaspoon bicarbonate of soda
50 g (2 oz) butter
100 g (4 oz) light brown sugar
1 egg
175 g (6 oz) self-raising flour
pinch of salt
½ teaspoon ground mixed spice
Syrup:
150 ml (¼ pint) water
50 g (2 oz) light brown sugar
large knob of butter
½ teaspoon vanilla essence
3 tablespoons brandy

Preparation time: 20 minutes
Cooking time: 45 minutes
Oven: 180°C, 350°F, Gas Mark 4

1. Put the dates, boiling water and bicarbonate of soda in a basin. Mix and leave to one side.
2. Cream the butter and sugar until pale, then beat in the egg. Sift the dry ingredients together and beat into the creamed mixture alternately with the dates and their liquid.
3. Spoon the mixture into a greased 1.2 litre (2 pint) ovenproof serving dish and bake in a preheated oven for 45 minutes until risen and golden.
4. Just before the pudding is ready, place all the ingredients for the syrup in a saucepan. Heat slowly until the sugar is dissolved, then bring to the boil.
5. Prick the pudding all over the surface with a skewer. Pour the boiling syrup over the leave for 5 minutes to absorb. Serve at once with ice cream or fresh cream.

FROZEN DESSERTS

LEMON ICE CREAM

Serves 8
grated rind of 2 lemons
juice of 3 lemons
175 g (6 oz) caster sugar
1 x 300 ml (10 fl oz) carton double cream
300 ml (½ pint) milk
angelica leaves, to decorate

Preparation time: 15 minutes, plus freezing

1. Place the lemon rind, juice and sugar in a mixing bowl. Stir well. Add the cream and whisk until thickened enough to show the trail of the whisk.
2. Slowly whisk in the milk. Transfer to a large container and freeze until 'slushy'.
3. Place the ice cream in a large bowl. Whisk until smooth and return to the freezer, either in individual ramekin dishes or one large container.
4. Decorate with angelica leaves and if preferred, serve with fresh raspberries.

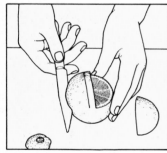
Forming a handle.

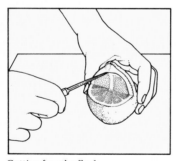
Cutting free the flesh.

ICED ZABAGLIONE

Serves 6-8
6 egg yolks
6 tablespoons caster sugar
6 tablespoons Marsala
200 ml (⅓ pint) double or whipping cream
To decorate:
whipped cream
crystallized violets and/or angelica leaves.

Preparation time: 10 minutes, plus cooling
Cooking time: 10 minutes

STRAWBERRY WATER ICE

75 g (3 oz) sugar
250 ml (8 fl oz) water
1½ teaspoons lemon juice
275 g (10 oz) strawberries, puréed
1 egg white
1½ tablespoons icing sugar, sieved

Preparation time: 10 minutes, plus freezing
Cooking time: 5 minutes

1. Dissolve the sugar in the water over gentle heat. Bring to the boil and boil rapidly for 3 minutes. Cool.
2. Stir in the lemon juice and strawberry purée and pour into a freezer container. Freeze until 'slushy'.
3. Whisk the egg white until stiff, whisk in the icing sugar. Whisk this into the strawberry mixture until evenly combined. Return to the container and freeze until solid.
4. To serve, use a melon baller to form small scoops.

Variation:
This recipe may be adapted to use any soft fruits or any fruit purée of your choice. Start with 300 ml (½ pint) unsweetened fruit purée and continue according to the recipe. For an attractive presentation, serve 2-3 different flavours at one time decorated with a little of the fresh fruits used. For example, serve pear, strawberry and raspberry water ices with pear slices, and one or two raspberries and strawberries. Another idea is to spoon over a little liqueur before serving, for example, blackcurrant water ice with Crème de Cassis.

1. Combine the egg yolks, sugar and Marsala in a large basin. Place over a pan of simmering water and whisk until thick and pale, about 10 minutes.
2. Remove from the heat and continue whisking for 5 minutes until cool.
3. Whip the cream until it stands in soft peaks. Fold into the cool egg mixture.
4. Spoon into ramekin dishes and freeze until required. Decorate with cream, violets and/or angelica leaves.
5. For special occasions, scoop the flesh out of lemons to make baskets and fill these with zabaglione. Freeze as above.

Strawberry water ice; Iced zabaglione; Lemon ice cream

CHESTNUT LOG

Serves 10-12
225 g (8 oz) plain chocolate polka dots
175 g (6 oz) butter
1 x 440 g (15½ oz) can chestnut purée
2 eggs
150 g (5 oz) caster sugar
2 tablespoons brandy
To decorate:
plain chocolate, melted
marrons glacé

Preparation time: 20 minutes
Cooking time: 2-3 minutes

1. Place half the chocolate and butter in a basin over hot water until melted. Cut the chestnut purée into small pieces and beat into the chocolate mixture.
2. Whisk the eggs and sugar until thick and pale. Whisk into the chocolate mixture. Stir in the brandy, then the remaining chocolate polka dots.
3. Transfer the mixture to a 1 kg (2 lb) loaf tin and freeze until solid. If preferred, when firm enough, place the mixture on a large piece of foil and roll into a log shape.
4. Unmould on to a serving plate. Decorate with piped melted chocolate and marrons glacé and leave to soften at room temperature for about 30 minutes.

CHOCOLATE RUM CAKE

Serves 12-14
225 g (8 oz) butter
225 g (8 oz) plain chocolate
100 g (4 oz) caster sugar
3 eggs
100 g (4 oz) maraschino cherries, well drained
100 g (4 oz) mixed nuts (walnuts, toasted almonds and hazelnuts), roughly chopped
2 tablespoons dark rum
225 g (8 oz) plain sweet biscuits, roughly broken

Preparation time: 20 minutes
Cooking time: 5 minutes

1. Grease and bottom line a 1 kg (2 lb) loaf tin.
2. Melt the butter and chocolate together in a saucepan over gentle heat. Allow to cool.
3. Place the sugar and eggs in a bowl and whisk together until pale and thick. Fold in the chocolate mixture, and then add the remaining ingredients. Spoon the mixture into the preared tin, cover and freeze.
4. To serve, unmould on to a serving plate and allow to soften in the refrigerator for about 30 minutes. Cut into slices.

PRALINE ICE CREAM

Serves 6
1 x 300 ml (10 fl oz) carton single cream
1 egg
2 egg yolks
75 g (3 oz) caster sugar
1 x 300 ml (10 fl oz) carton double or whipping cream
Praline:
75 g (3 oz) caster sugar
75 g (3 oz) whole unblanched almonds

Preparation time: 45 minutes, plus freezing
Cooking time: 25-30 minutes

1. Heat the single cream to just below boiling point.
2. Whisk the egg, egg yolks and sugar together. Stir in the hot cream and place in a basin over a pan of hot water on the heat. Stir frequently, until the custard is thick enough to coat the back of a wooden spoon, about 20 minutes.
3. Strain into a suitable freezer container and freeze for several hours until 'slushy'.
4. Meanwhile, make the praline; place the sugar and almonds in a saucepan over medium heat until the sugar caramelizes. Do not stir. Pour the mixture onto a buttered baking sheet and leave until cold. Either grate in a rotary grater or grind in a coffee grinder.
5. Remove the egg custard from the freezer. Beat until smooth. Whip the cream until it stands in soft peaks. Fold into the custard with three-quarters of the praline. Return to the container and freeze until solid.
6. To serve, scoop spoonfuls into a serving dish and sprinkle with extra praline.

Variation:
To make Brown Bread Ice Cream, omit the praline. Toast 100 g (4 oz) good quality wholemeal or granary breadcrumbs until crisp. Allow to go cold and fold into the custard with the whipped cream. Continue as above. Decorate with crystallized violets.

Chestnut log; Praline ice cream; Chocolate rum cake

FLORIDA MUD PIE

Serves 6

200 g (7 oz) chocolate digestive biscuits, crushed
65 g (2½ oz) butter, melted
1 tablespoon cocoa powder
½ litre (18 fl oz) coffee ice cream

Sauce:

75 g (3 oz) soft brown sugar
50 g (2 oz) butter
300 ml (½ pint) milk
100 g (4 oz) dark chocolate
few drops of vanilla essence
2 teaspoons cornflour
1 tablespoon water

To decorate:

1 x 300 ml (10 fl oz) carton double or whipping cream,
   whipped
grated chocolate or chocolate curls (page 16)

Preparation time: 20 minutes, plus freezing

This is a simple ice cream dessert served with a warm chocolate fudge sauce.

1. Combine the biscuit crumbs, butter and cocoa powder and use to line the base and sides of a 20 cm (8 inch) flan tin. Chill until firm.

2. Fill the flan case with coffee ice cream. Place in the freezer.

3. To make the sauce, melt the sugar in a saucepan over medium heat and allow to caramelize a little. Stir in the butter, then the milk, chocolate and vanilla essence and simmer until the chocolate is melted.

4. Mix the cornflour and water, add to the chocolate sauce and simmer gently until thickened.

5. Remove the flan from the freezer, pipe or spoon whipped cream on top and decorate with chocolate. Serve with the warm chocolate fudge sauce.

COFFEE AND HAZELNUT ICE CREAM CAKE

Serves 6-8

450 ml (¾ pint) single cream
1 egg
3 egg yolks
100 g (4 oz) caster sugar
40 g (1½ oz) ground coffee
150 ml (¼ pint) boiling water
50 g (2 oz) icing sugar
450 ml (¾ pint) double or whipping cream
50 g (2 oz) roasted hazelnuts, ground

To decorate:

whipped cream
chocolate 'coffee beans' or roasted hazelnuts

Preparation time: about 1½ hours, plus freezing
Cooking time: 35 minutes

Chocolate 'coffee beans' can be bought from confectioners and delicatessens.

1. Chill a 1.2 litre (2 pint) bombe mould in the freezer overnight.
2. Bring the single cream just to the boil. Beat together the egg, egg yolks and caster sugar. Stir in the hot cream.
3. Strain into a basin set over hot water and cook until the custard is thick enough to coat the back of a wooden spoon. Transfer one third of the custard to a separate bowl.
4. Mix the coffee and boiling water. Leave to infuse for 15 minutes, then strain. Stir in the icing sugar.
5. Stir the coffee into the larger quantity of custard, cool then freeze both portions for about 1 hour until 'slushy'.
6. Beat each portion of custard to an even consistency.
7. Whip the double cream until it forms soft peaks. Fold two-thirds of the cream into the coffee mixture. Fold the remaining cream into the plain custard and stir in the hazelnuts. Refreeze both portions for about 1 hour.
8. Beat both mixtures again. Return the hazelnut ice cream to the freezer. With the back of a tablespoon spread the coffee ice cream evenly around the sides and bottom of the chilled bombe mould, reserving sufficient ice cream to cover the top of the mould later. Return the mould and the remaining ice cream to the freezer and leave until solid.
9. Beat the hazelnut ice cream and spoon it into the mould, leaving a 5 mm (¼ inch) gap at the top. Freeze again until solid.
10. Beat the reserved coffee ice cream and fill the mould to the top. Cover with an oiled circle of greaseproof paper and the mould lid. Freeze until solid.
11. To serve, unmould the bombe on to a plate. Decorate with rosettes of whipped cream, chocolate 'coffee beans' or roasted hazelnuts.

ICED LEMON PIE

Serves 6
175 g (6 oz) digestive biscuits, crushed
75 g (3 oz) butter, melted
Filling:
2 eggs, separated
grated rind of 1 lemon
4 tablespoons lemon juice
100 ml (3½ fl oz) condensed milk
2 tablespoons caster sugar
To decorate:
whipped cream
finely shredded lemon rind

Preparation time: 25 minutes, plus freezing

1. Mix the biscuit crumbs and butter and use to line the base and sides of a 20 cm (8 inch) flan dish or tin. Chill until firm.
2. Whisk the egg yolks until pale. Stir in the lemon rind and juice and the condensed milk.
3. Whisk the egg whites until stiff, then whisk in the sugar. Fold into the lemon mixture and spoon into the prepared biscuit case. Freeze until required.
4. Decorate the top with small scoops or piped whirls of cream and lemon shreds.

CHOCOLATE AND ORANGE CUPS

Serves 6
100 g (4 oz) plain chocolate, melted
6 tablespoons double or whipping cream
2 tablespoons plain unsweetened yogurt
6 tablespoons orange curd
crystallized orange peel, to decorate

Preparation time: 25 minutes, plus chilling

1. Working 1 at a time, pour a little melted chocolate into 6 foil cup cases. Carefully brush the chocolate up the sides of the cases. Chill until firm, then repeat. Chill again until solid. Carefully peel away the foil cases. Freeze.
2. Whip the cream until firm, then stir in the yogurt and the orange curd. Spoon into the prepared chocolate cases and swirl the top.
3. Decorate each cup with fine strips of crystallized orange peel. Freeze until required.

 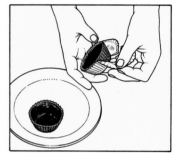

Brushing with chocolate.   Peeling away the foil cases.

Chocolate and orange cups

Stem ginger sundaes

STEM GINGER SUNDAES

Serves 6
1 quantity Praline ice cream (page 72), see method
Ginger Horns:
25 g (1 oz) butter
25 g (1 oz) caster sugar
1 tablespoon golden syrup
25 g (1 oz) plain flour
¼ teaspoon ground ginger
1½ teaspoons brandy
To Decorate:
1 x 150 ml (¼ pint) double cream, whipped
12 small pieces stem ginger

Preparation time: about 1½ hours, plus freezing and cooling
Cooking time: 1 hour
Oven: 180°C, 350°F, Gas Mark 4

1. Prepare Praline ice cream following the recipe (page 72) but omit the praline and add 75 g (3 oz) stem ginger.
2. To make the ginger horns, place the butter, sugar and golden syrup in a saucepan. Stir over a gentle heat until melted. Remove from the heat and stir in the remaining ingredients.
3. Spoon teaspoonfuls of the mixture well apart on to greased baking sheets. Use 2 baking sheets with 2 biscuits on each.
4. Bake in a preheated oven for 8-10 minutes, until golden. Allow to cool for a few seconds, then roll around horn-shaped tins. Place on a wire tray until cold, then remove the tins. Continue until 12 horns are made.
5. To assemble the sundaes, pipe a whirl of cream into the top of each horn. Top with a piece of stem ginger. Place 2 horns and a large scoop of ice cream in each of 6 dishes. Serve at once.

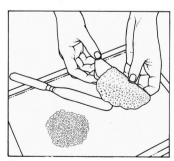

Shaping the biscuits.

Removing the mould.

IGLOO PUDDING

Serves 6-8
50 g (2 oz) raisins
25 g (1 oz) sultanas
25 g (1 oz) currants
50 g (2 oz) maraschino cherries, quartered
50 g (2 oz) blanched almonds, toasted and chopped
2 tablespoons medium sherry
1 x 125 g (4½ oz) packet marshmallows
150 ml (¼ pint) milk
1 tablespoon instant coffee powder
1 tablespoon cocoa powder
1 x 300 ml (10 fl oz) carton double or whipping cream

Preparation time: 15 minutes, plus soaking
Cooking time: 2-3 minutes

1. Place the raisins, sultanas, currants, cherries, almonds and sherry in a bowl. Leave to soak for 1 hour.
2. Place the marshmallows, milk, coffee and cocoa powder in a saucepan, and heat gently until the marshmallows are melted. Allow to cool.
3. Whip the cream until stiff, whisk in the marshmallow mixture, then fold in the fruit mixture and sherry.
4. Turn into a 1.4 litres (2¼ pint) pudding basin. Cover and freeze until solid. Unmould when required.

BISCUIT TORTONI

Serves 6-8
2 egg whites
4 tablespoons caster sugar
1 x 300 ml (10 fl oz) carton double or whipping cream
175 g (6 oz) blanched almonds, toasted and roughly chopped
4 tablespoons Amaretto liqueur

LEMON FREEZER LOAF

Serves 8
225 g (8 oz) butter
225 g (8 oz) icing sugar
grated rind and juice of 2 large lemons
2 eggs, separated
200 ml (⅓ pint) double cream
2 tablespoons Marsala or medium sherry
1 packet trifle sponge cakes
To decorate:
whipped cream
lemon rind, grated
angelica leaves

Preparation time: 15 minutes

1. Cream the butter, 175 g (6 oz) of the sugar and the lemon rind until light and fluffy. Beat in the egg yolks 1 at a time, then beat in half the lemon juice.
2. Whisk the cream until it forms soft peaks and fold into the lemon butter. Whisk the egg whites until stiff and fold them into the mixture.
3. Mix the reserved lemon juice with the Marsala. Split the trifle sponges in half, arrange 4 pieces on the base of a 900 g (2 lb) loaf tin and sprinkle with a little Marsala and lemon juice. Spoon in one-third of the lemon mixture. Continue in layers finishing with sponge cake. Freeze until required.
4. Transfer to a serving plate, decorate with whipped cream rosettes, grated lemon rind and angelica leaves. Allow to soften in the refrigerator for about 30 minutes.

Preparation time: 20 minutes, plus freezing

1. Whisk the egg whites until stiff. Whisk in the sugar a tablespoon at a time until thick and glossy.
2. Whip the cream to soft peaks, then fold into the egg white mixture with 75 g (3 oz) chopped almonds and the Amaretto liqueur.
3. Spoon into a 1.2 litre (2 pint) loaf tin, cover and freeze.
4. Unmould on to a serving plate. Press the remaining almonds over the surfaces of the loaf until completely covered. Freeze again until required.

Biscuit Tortoni; Igloo pudding

INDEX

PDO 83-203